The First-Year Experience Cookbook

edited by Raymond Pun and Meggan Houlihan

Association of College and Research Libraries
A division of the American Library Association

Chicago • 2017

The paper used in this publication meets the minimum requirements of American National Standard for Information Sciences-Permanence of Paper for Printed Library Materials, ANSI Z39.48-1992. ∞

The ACRL Cookbook series was conceived of and designed by Ryan Sittler and Doug Cook.

Other books in this series:
The Library Instruction Cookbook by Ryan L. Sittler and Douglas Cook
The Embedded Librarian's Cookbook edited by Kaijsa Calkins and Cassandra Kvenild
The Discovery Tool Cookbook: Recipes for Successful Lesson Plans edited by Nancy Fawley and Nikki Krysak

Library of Congress Cataloging-in-Publication Data

Names: Pun, Raymond, 1985- editor. | Houlihan, Meggan, editor.
Title: The first-year experience cookbook / edited by Raymond Pun and Meggan
   Houlihan.
Description: Chicago : Association of College and Research Libraries, a
   division of the American Library Association, 2017.
Identifiers: LCCN 2017000404 | ISBN 9780838989203 (pbk.)
Subjects: LCSH: Library orientation for college students. | Library
   orientation for college students--United States--Case studies. | College
   freshmen--Services for. | Information literacy--Study and teaching
   (Higher) | Instruction librarians. | Academic libraries--Relations with
   faculty and curriculum.
Classification: LCC Z711.25.C65 F57 2017 | DDC 025.5/677--dc23 LC record available at https://lccn.loc.
gov/2017000404

Printed in the United States of America.
21 20 19 18 17   5 4 3 2 1

TABLE OF CONTENTS

Table of Contents

Table of Contents

Acknowledgements

We would like to thank all contributors who submitted high-quality recipes for this book!

We would also like to thank ACRL for supporting our cookbook proposal and helping us make this idea become a reality.

How to Contact Us
Raymond Pun
First Year Student Success Librarian
California State University, Fresno
raypun@csufresno.edu

Meggan Houlihan
First-Year Experience and Instruction Librarian
New York University Abu Dhabi
mah23@nyu.edu

INTRODUCTION

Introduction

Raymond Pun, First Year Student Success Librarian, California State University, Fresno, raypun@csufresno.edu; Meggan Houlihan, First-Year Experience and Instruction Librarian, New York University Abu Dhabi, mah23@nyu.edu

First-year students often face many challenges related to adjusting to university life, including making the most of the university library. Librarians are constantly addressing student misconceptions about libraries and locating information. We've also been working hard to better reach our first-year students and create high impact practices in student retention. Through a number of committees, such as the RUSA First-Year Experience interest group and ACRL's FYE interest group, and publishing best practices for teaching first-year students, we're making headway.

The cookbook was designed to provide librarians with a series of innovative approaches to teaching and assessing information literacy skills during the first year. The volume compiles a list of recipes for you to adapt, repurpose, and implement in your libraries. Four major categories are addressed in this cookbook: orientations, library instruction, programs, and assessment.

PART I: ORIENTATIONS

Library orientation is often the first point of contact between first-year students and library staff, resources, and services. We felt this crucial interaction was deserving of its own chapter, and the large number of recipe proposals we considered supported this initial idea. There are two subchapters:

General Orientation covers timeless activities for your general first-year population; and Special Orientation covers activities for specific groups of students, such as transfer, international, and honors students.

PART II: LIBRARY INSTRUCTION

From addressing the ACRL Framework in first-year classes to innovative active learning techniques, this chapter focuses on library instructional services for first-year students. Sub-chapter topics include instruction for general first-year courses and instruction for discipline-specific courses. Librarians provide numerous examples of successfully incorporating the ACRL Framework into courses and your daily instructional practices. The discipline-based instruction sub-chapter provides examples of information literacy in business, engineering, and STEM courses.

PART III: PROGRAMS

Unlike the Library Instruction chapter, this chapter focuses specifically on engaging students through programmatic efforts and activities. Programs are divided into two categories: First-Year Experience (FYE) programs and general library programs. The FYE program offers examples of how libraries have partnered with first-year seminars, FYE programs, learning communities, or academic departments to foster greater

collaborations. The library program provides recipes on creative practices related to student engagement in the library.

PART IV: ASSESSMENT

A quick taste test of this chapter reveals thought-provoking, innovative ways to assess library services, programs, and instruction targeted at first-year students. This chapter is broken down into two separate sub-chapters: Instructional Assessment, which focuses on assessing student learning, and First-Year Experience Assessment, which focuses on assessing the general library experience of first-year students. From ethnography research, to one-shot assessment plans to focus groups, this chapter will help you prepare librarians for designing and implementing a first-year assessment plan.

Remember, the lesson plans, programs, and assessment activities in this book should not be limited to first-year students. Whether you're working with high school or graduate students, these innovative activities can be adopted and repurposed, which is highly encouraged! Be creative. Think big! Collaborate with campus partners, such as Student Affairs, the Writing Center, academic programs, and athletics, to create the most effective first-year information literacy programs for your students.

PART I. ORIENTATIONS

General and Special Orientations

How Sweet it is!
Making Library Orientations Palatable Again with Library Mythbusters

Chapel D. Cowden, Health & Science Librarian, University of Tennessee at Chattanooga, Chapel-Cowden@utc.edu

NUTRITION INFORMATION

Library Mythbusters is designed to be a flexible, engaging orientation to a library and its services. With a frame (the Mythbusters TV show) to hang the activity on, students are immediately engaged to participate because they have a pop cultural connection to the activity. Library Mythbusters can be remixed and reused for virtually any orientation—from first-year students, to transfers, to graduate students, or anyone new to the library and its services.

NUMBERS SERVED

Any number of students can participate in this activity.

COOKING TIME

Library Mythbusters can be completed in as little as 7–10 minutes, but can easily be extended or reduced depending upon the desired amount of information coverage.

DIETARY GUIDELINES

Providing new students with the opportunity to explore the physical and intellectual spaces of the library in a non-threatening environment is a critical introduction to the role that the library assumes on a college campus. In this activity, students are not simply told about the library spaces and ser-

vices, but are asked to construct meaning and contribute knowledge through providing their own experiences with the library.

MAIN INGREDIENTS

- ☐ Instructor's podium (computer, projector)
- ☐ Prezi or PowerPoint for displaying "myths"
- ☐ A set of "myth" cards for the students
- ☐ Participation prizes (optional)

MAIN COOKING TECHNIQUE

Discussion

PREPARATION

- ☐ Determine what needs to be covered in the orientation and create learning objectives.
- ☐ Create a slide deck with one image per slide and the text "Myth?" on the slide. These are the visuals that correspond to the "myths." Some will be true, also known as "confirmed" in Mythbusters lingo, and some will be false, or "busted." A third option is to have "plausible" myths. Within the slide deck, an animation needs to be added to each slide that drops in the words "Plausible," "Confirmed," or "Busted" after the students determine

the status of the "myth." A freely available *Mythbusters* show font is widely available for download.

- ☐ Using the slide deck images, create corresponding cards on card stock with "myth" statements. An example myth includes a stereotypic image of a librarian with the statement, "Librarians love to shush people. And they all wear buns. And glasses. And they are mean…and lonely." This myth will then prompt a discussion of the role of a librarian and ways a librarian can help—research consults, chat service, reference desk help, etc.
- ☐ (Optional) Prizes are not necessary, but are useful in getting students to participate in reading a card if they seem timid.

MAIN COOKING TECHNIQUE

1. Have the slide deck ready to go when students enter the classroom.
2. Give a brief introduction about the *Mythbusters* show and how it relates to the game. Something to the tune of "Has anyone seen the show *Mythbusters*?" Usually, everyone has. If not, give a one- to two-sentence description.
3. Provide instructions to students:
   a. "I'm going to hand out cards,

each of which has an image and a 'myth'." Hand out cards.

b. "When you see the slide with the same image as the one on your card, read the 'myth' on your card to the class."

c. "As a class, guess whether the myth is true (confirmed), false (busted), or possible (plausible)."

4. After each myth is read, prompt the class as to whether they think it is true or false and why.

5. After students decide the "truth," provide the answer and discuss the corresponding service or concept.

6. After all myths are read and discussed, take up cards and hand out prizes (if using).

ALLERGY WARNINGS

- Like any activity, this can get old if you do it semester after semester. Spice it up by changing up slide decks and myths every couple of semesters.

- It is also important to try to avoid using it in classes with students who have likely already encountered it.

CHEF'S NOTE

I originally created this activity for use in a nursing student orientation. We now use it as a combined icebreaker and library orientation for all our Freshman English Composition classes. It is also widely used in other classes for transfer students, ESL students, master's and doctoral students, and in any other class where a library orientation is necessary. Library Mythbusters has proved to be so flexible and engaging for such a wide array of students that we have no plans to put it on the backburner any time soon.

ADDITIONAL RESOURCES

One of the many slide decks and card sets can be accessed from the following website: http://www.utc.edu/library/services/instruction/teaching-materials/library-mythbusters.php. Please feel free to remix and reuse for your own purposes!

Find Your #FlatLibrarian:
Using an Instagram Photo Booth to Introduce Students to Subject-Specialist Liaison Librarians

Elizabeth Rugan Shepard, Instruction Coordinator Librarian, University of South Alabama, erugan@southalabama.edu

NUTRITION INFORMATION

Librarians who regularly interact with first-year students know all too well that these newly minted college students experience quite the learning curve when it comes to academic libraries. They struggle with the labyrinthian spaces of the library and its hieroglyphic call number system, but more troubling to librarians than general space orientation issues is the fact that many of these students spend their entire college career unaware of the personnel resources available to them in the library. Like most academic libraries, our library has subject-specialist liaison librarians assigned to support research in certain disciplines based on their knowledge or education. We wanted students to be aware that these subject-specialist liaison librarians exist and to know—literally recognize—the face of their potential major's librarian.

Hosted during freshman orientation campus activities, the Find Your #FlatLibrarian Instagram Photo Booth is a fun, social way to introduce students to "their" liaison librarian. The photo booth is stocked with fun props and flat librarians—hand fans that feature the liaison librarians' headshots. Based on their major or potential major, students locate their librarian on a poster, dress up in crazy props, and snap a pic with that flat librarian. (Something to keep in mind: these students are freshmen and most are undeclared, but many have an idea of their potential major). These photos are posted to the library's Instagram account for everyone who follows to see how cool your library is (*Library Marketing Plug*: We did encourage students to tag themselves in the photos so that they showed up in their feeds—more free advertising of your awesomeness.)

NUMBERS SERVED

Accommodates as many students as are willing to participate.

COOKING TIME

- Preparation Time: 4–5 hours
- Cook Time (actual event): 3 hours

DIETARY GUIDELINES

In creating an activity that encourages students to identify "their" liaison librarian, we are developing in students a disposition to seek appropriate help when needed. The #flatlibrarian photo booth is a quick and fun way to introduce students to the idea that disciplines have specific and different research needs while also "introducing" the students to the person who will help them navigate those research expectations.

ACRL FRAMEWORK ADDRESSED

Research as Inquiry

MAIN INGREDIENTS

- ☐ Two librarians
- ☐ Advertisements
- ☐ Liaison librarian poster
- ☐ Liaison librarian fans
- ☐ Fabric backdrop
- ☐ Funny props (e.g. cowboy hat, feather boa, etc.)
- ☐ Library swag
- ☐ Candy
- ☐ 2 iPads logged into the library's Instagram account

PREPARATION

- ☐ Design, print, and post flyers advertising the activity.
- ☐ Create a poster with the headshots of all liaison librarians and their assigned disciplines.
- ☐ Put together #flatlibrarian fans. It's a good idea to use the same headshot here as appears on the poster. You can do this on the cheap by printing out librarian headshots, gluing them to cardboard, and then taping free paint stirrers from a home improvement store to the back to make a fan.

☐ Gather supplies for photo booth. Shop for props and candy. Gather swag.

☐ Assemble photo booth. Hang back drop and poster. Set out props, #flatlibrarians, and candy. Charge iPads and log in to library Instagram account.

☐ Turn up some tunes and prepare to have a blast!

MAIN COOKING METHOD

1. No complicated ingredient combinations here; just set up your photo booth and wait for the students to come.

2. Once they arrive, have one librarian explain what a liaison librarian is, assist students in locating their librarian based on their major or potential major on the poster, and find that corresponding #flatlibrarian. Encourage the student(s) to dress up in the crazy props (Note: little encouragement is needed).

3. The second librarian serves as the photographer. Once students have had their pics taken, pass the iPad to the student(s) to apply any filters, create their own caption, and tag themselves. Before you post the photo, be sure to add the hashtag #flatlibrarian.

ALLERGY WARNINGS

- No Michelin-rated chefs needed for this orientation activity; it's pretty un-complicated! Only warning: Do ask fun and excited librarians to staff the photo booth.

- You do want to encourage student engagement, so it's best to choose librarians who won't hesitate to grab a foam finger!

CHEF'S NOTE

Although this activity is really fun and seems a bit silly (there are oversized cowboy hats involved after all), our library has seen some significant benefits from the event. Most are related to student perception of the library; students at the event and later have noted to library staff how fun and "un-library" the activity was (because we all know how dusty and dull libraries are…). Additionally, our liaison librarians have noted that the photo booth achieved its goal—students recognize and seek out their librarians for research assistance.

ADDITIONAL RESOURCES

Check out our #flatlibrarian photo booth @ marx.library

The Magnificent Library Race

Katherine O'Clair, Agriculture and Environmental Sciences Librarian, California Polytechnic State University, koclair@calpoly.edu

NUTRITION INFORMATION

The Magnificent Library Race provides an engaging and interactive way to teach introductory library skills and concepts to first-year students. Students respond well to the competitive nature of this activity, which translates into a positive library learning experience. The Magnificent Library Race can be adapted to fit any course or subject area, making it usable for both general education and discipline specific courses.

NUMBERS SERVED

Works best for groups of 15–40 students

COOKING TIME

Varies; can be any duration from 50 to 120 minutes

DIETARY GUIDELINES

This activity provides an interactive, hands-on, team-based learning experience for students to learn basic library skills and information literacy concepts. It provides a foundation for students to develop more discipline-specific and sophisticated research and information literacy skills.

MAIN INGREDIENTS

☐ Computer lab or access to devices with internet access

☐ Small (recloseable) envelopes

☐ Question sheets for each team and leg of the race (color coded for each leg)

☐ Answer sheets for students to fill in as they complete the race legs

☐ Promotional materials or other "goodies" that can be awarded as prizes

☐ LibGuide or other research guide, if desired

MAIN COOKING TECHNIQUE

Active, hands-on, team-based learning

PREPARATION

☐ Establish the race topics or themes (e.g., about the library, searching for books, formatting citations) for each leg of the race.
  » Four to six legs are recommended.

☐ Create the questions for each leg (see Figure 1).
  » You want students to get adequate experience with the topic or theme, so include the optimal number of questions (generally 4–6) to achieve this in the shortest amount of time.
  » Questions should require students to use a library-related resource (e.g., library website, catalog, discovery tool) to determine the correct answer.

☐ Identify the number of students that will attend the session. Use this number to establish (roughly) the number of teams and students (3–5) in each team.
  » Need to be as equal in size as possible for fairness.
  » Teams can be assigned or students can form their own teams.
  » No more than eight teams is recommended.

☐ Copy the question sheets (use colored paper for each leg) and package the questions for each team for each leg of the race.
  » For example, if you have six legs and six teams, you will have 36 envelopes with question sheets.

☐ Prepare the answer sheets for students to complete (see Figure 2). Each student will complete their own answer sheet.

☐ Prepare the master answer sheet that will be used to verify students' answers.

☐ Gather the prizes that will be awarded to the winning team(s).
  » One grand prize, or
  » Prizes for first, second, and third place teams.
  » Consolation prizes for all participants (small promotional item) are recommended, too.

COOKING METHOD

1. Form the race teams as recommended above.
2. Assign students (or teams) to a computer or device with internet access.
3. Ask each team to come up with a unique team name (just for fun!).
4. Ask each team to select a captain that will present the master answer sheet for verification of correct answers upon completion of each leg.
5. Pass out answer sheets to all students (each student must complete their own answer sheet to receive credit for the activity).
6. Direct students to the library website, guide, or other resources that will be used to find answers to the questions.
    a. Demonstrate resources as needed to allow for self-directed investigation.
7. Pass out the Leg One envelopes to each team.
8. Start the Magnificent Library Race!
9. As student teams complete the questions, the team captain will present the team's answer sheets for verification.
10. Teams will only move on to the next leg if they have answered ALL the questions correctly.
    a. If they have not, provide a hint or two and send them back to their team to try again.
11. Collect that leg's question sheet and envelopes (for later reuse).
12. Give the next leg's questions to the team captain.
13. Repeat steps 9 through 12 above until each team has finished the race.
14. Award prizes to the top team(s).
15. Have the students turn in their answer sheets to their course instructor for participation credit (or as determined for your specific need).

ALLERGY WARNINGS

Instruct teams not to write on the question sheets, as you will reuse them. Teams that do will be disqualified from that race leg and will no longer be eligible to win or place in the race.

CHEF'S NOTE

This activity requires extensive preparation, especially during the initial development of the questions. Many of the questions can be easily adapted for a specific discipline. The question materials for this activity can be reused in future instances, which significantly reduces the preparation time in the future. Library student assistants can help with stuffing the envelopes for future sessions.

Carefully consider the amount of time you will have with the students when determining the number of legs for the race and the number of questions in each leg. You will want to make sure students can complete all the legs in the race. Don't forget the time you will need to verify their answers.

Keep the questions and the answers as straightforward as possible. Make sure the answers to the questions are absolute. There is a frenzy of activity during the session, and it will be difficult to explain complex or confusing topics during the race itself. Verifying the student teams' answer

---

FIGURE 1. EXAMPLE QUESTIONS

About the Library
- Where is the Research Help Desk located?
- What are course reserves?

Understanding Plagiarism
- What is [*your institution's*] definition of plagiarism?

Finding Books
- On which floor of the library is [*specific book*] located?

Finding Articles
- List the 3 types of articles and the audience for each type.
- List two databases you could use to find articles on topics related to your major.
- Create a search statement to find articles on [*specific topic*]. Use this to search [*specific database*] and list the title of a relevant article you find.

Citing Your Sources
- Is the following citation for a book or an article?
- Identify the [*journal title, article title, volume, issue*] in the following citation.

sheets requires time and attention, so ask questions that you can quickly assess as correct or incorrect answers. Ask the course instructor to assist you or consider utilizing a peer assistant.

ACKNOWLEDGEMENT
Thank you to Jennifer Duvernay for her vision and inspiration for the Magnificent Library Race.

Name_____Team_____

The Magnificent Library Race Answer Sheet

You will form teams of 4 or 5 people. Please select a name for your team and a team captain. Each team member will turn in his/her own worksheet, but you will be working together during the race. There are four legs of the race, and they are to be worked on one at a time. The answers for each leg must be completely correct before your team can go on to the next one. The team that finishes the race first will win a prize.

Leg #1–About the Library

1.

2.

3.

Leg #2–Citing Sources

1.

2.

3.

Leg #3–Books

1.

2.

Leg #4–Articles

1.

2.

3.

FIGURE 2. ANSWER SHEET

A Spoonful of Sugar:
Using Instagram and Kahoot to Sweeten Library Orientation

Elizabeth Marcus, Undergraduate Experience Librarian, Western Carolina University, emarcus@wcu.edu

NUTRITION INFORMATION

This recipe is a fun and interactive way to introduce students in First-Year Experience or transition courses to library services, resources, and personnel. The activity was created to fully engage students in the orientation process, as students and librarians were dissatisfied with the lecturing nature of traditional library tours. This recipe utilizes a social media platform and mobile learning game many students are already familiar with. These tools encourage visual learning and allow informal assessment of knowledge gained.

NUMBERS SERVED

Approximately 25 students

COOKING TIME

45 minutes

DIETARY GUIDELINES

The general purpose of this recipe is to support the academic success of first-year students, introducing them to the world of scholarly research.

ACRL FRAMEWORK ADDRESSED

- Information Has Value
- Research as Inquiry

MAIN INGREDIENTS

- ☐ Self-tour activity instruction handouts
- ☐ Library Instagram account
- ☐ Library or personal Kahoot account
- ☐ Smartphones or tablets with Instagram application (at least 1 device per student group)
- ☐ Instruction space with computer and connected TV monitor or projector

MAIN COOKING TECHNIQUE

Visual learning, game-based learning, group discussion

PREPARATION

- ☐ Think about which library services, resources, or concepts are crucial for students to know about in their first year. Produce a task list of related items, locations, or people for students to photograph that a librarian can briefly expound upon later (e.g., find the best study spot).
- ☐ Create an activity handout that includes the library's Instagram username and password, 1–3 photography tasks, and instructions for posting to Instagram that may include a preferred description, location, and/or hashtags (see example instruction sheet).
- ☐ Build a Kahoot quiz of 3–5 questions that reiterates the most important points of the activity (e.g., how can students get research help?). Include photos and videos for personalization.

COOKING METHOD

1. Divide the class into small groups of 3–5 students and give each an activity handout.
2. Provide a tablet for each group or ask a volunteer with a smartphone to log in to the library's Instagram account using the username and password provided.
3. Assign 10–15 minutes for exploration, and designate a specific time for everyone to meet again.
4. Return to the instruction space to review photos and ask students to discuss what they found. At this point, the librarian may elaborate on particular library resources and services.
5. Ask a student in each group with the smartphone or tablet to enter the web address https://kahoot.it/ and type the Game Pin Number displayed on the screen into their device.
6. Navigate through the quiz, offering additional information if a question is answered incorrectly.
7. Prizes may be offered to the winning team, but bragging rights are often a sufficient reward.

ALLERGY WARNINGS

- This activity is difficult to complete in classes with fewer than 10 students, as fewer photos taken provide less opportunity to discuss all that the library offers. It is important to confirm how many students will be visiting the library with the professor and adjust instructions accordingly.
- Avoid vague Instagram tasks (e.g., find something fun), as the photo results may not provide optimal teaching opportunities. Ask students to photograph a specific item or concept.
- As a courtesy, it is important to notify library personnel that students may request to take photos of them. Most librarians do not mind, but they are certainly not obligated to participate. Students may be directed to ask the librarian's permission and photograph an item related to their job duties if the individual declines (see example instruction sheet).

CHEF'S NOTE

This orientation recipe has proved to be overwhelmingly popular among Western Carolina University's first-year students. In summer 2015, of 148 students surveyed, 97 percent said their overall experience with this activity was "good" or "very good." Students suggested that more Instagram tasks be assigned to each group and alternative social media platforms, like Snapchat, be used.

Many students who participate in this orientation activity later follow the library's Instagram page, so this recipe provides a wonderful opportunity to market events, extended hours, new services, and resources.

ADDITIONAL RESOURCES

Kahoot: https://kahoot.it/#/

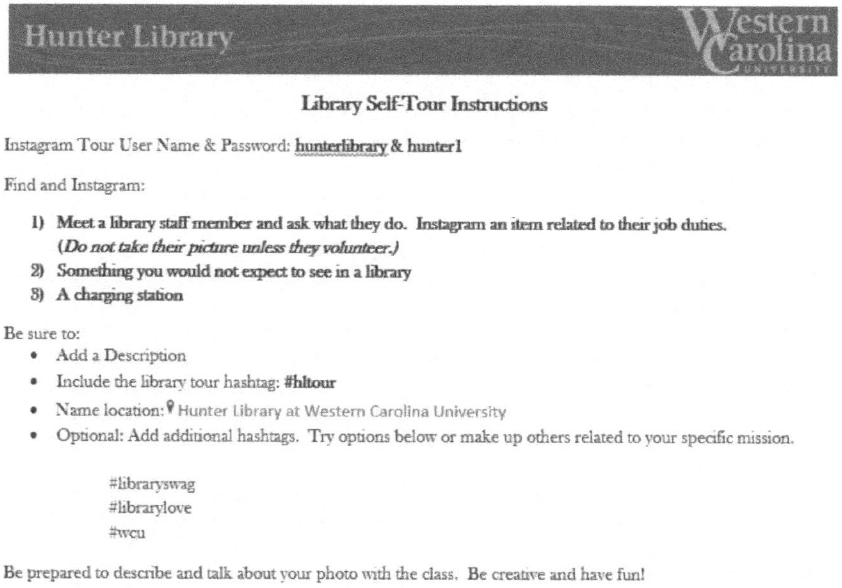

Hunter Library — Western Carolina University

Library Self-Tour Instructions

Instagram Tour User Name & Password: **hunterlibrary & hunter1**

Find and Instagram:

1) **Meet a library staff member and ask what they do. Instagram an item related to their job duties.** ***(Do not take their picture unless they volunteer.)***
2) **Something you would not expect to see in a library**
3) **A charging station**

Be sure to:

- Add a Description
- Include the library tour hashtag: **#hltour**
- Name location: Hunter Library at Western Carolina University
- Optional: Add additional hashtags. Try options below or make up others related to your specific mission.

#libraryswag
#librarylove
#wcu

Be prepared to describe and talk about your photo with the class. Be creative and have fun!

FIGURE 1. LIBRARY WEBSITE

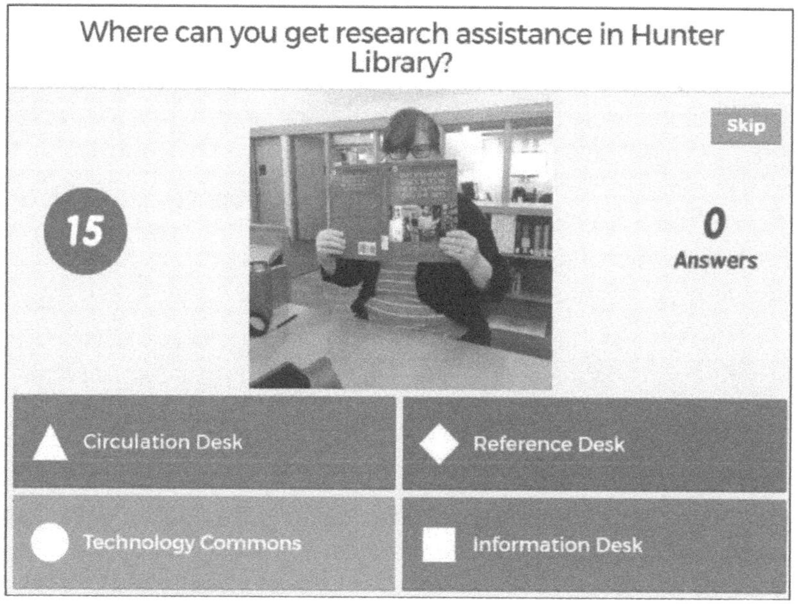

FIGURE 2. KAHOOT

Plateau de Fruits de Bibliothèque:
A Pictorial Scavenger Hunt Appetizer for Up-Close Students (Incoming Students)
Leila June Rod-Welch, Outreach Services Librarian & Associate Professor of Library Services, University of Northern Iowa, leila.rod-welch@uni.edu

NUTRITION INFORMATION
Learning outcomes and nutrition facts:
- Vitamin A: Familiarize students with the library's space.
- Vitamin B: Familiarize students with the library's resources and its services.
- Vitamin C: Lessen anxiety and help students feel comfortable asking questions.

This recipe will introduce basic library resources to incoming students. This session will help incoming students become familiar with the library's resources, services, and space; make them feel comfortable asking questions; and reduce the anxiety level that some of these students may have about using an academic library. Students who participate in this photographic scavenger hunt will be one step ahead of their peers when they start classes.

NUMBERS SERVED
Unlimited

COOKING TIME
Preparation time: 60 minutes. Preparation time for future events would be approximately 20 minutes.

Most students take approximately 45 minutes to complete the pictorial scavenger hunt. The cooking time can be tweaked based on your allotted time frame and the size of your library.

ACRL FRAMEWORK ADDRESSED
Searching as Strategic Exploration

MAIN INGREDIENTS
- ☐ 10 to 20 questions pertaining to library resources and services
- ☐ Camera or camera equipped smart device (phone or tablet)
- ☐ One or more librarians, library staff, or student assistants

MAIN COOKING TECHNIQUE
The main cooking technique used in this recipe is active learning, whereby students engage in an activity. In this particular case, students are engaged in a fun pictorial scavenger hunt to learn more about our library's space, resources, and its services.

PREPARATION
This recipe does not require too much advance preparation and it can be reused with minimal modifications for other occasions and audiences. The chef needs to prepare questions about different library resources, collections, and services available to students. This scavenger hunt differs from traditional scavenger hunts. In lieu of written answers, participants take pictures of their answers with a camera or smart device. Participants can be creative and take a selfie with the answers if they wish to do so. For example, in our library we have a display of world flags in a specific collection geared toward learners of English as a Second Language, and participants can take their selfies with the flags.

COOKING METHOD
1. Advertise the scavenger hunt in the list of activities available for student participation in their campus tour program through the Office of Admissions. As a librarian, ensure that your event's description is eye-catching. Remember, the library may be competing with other departments offering sessions at the same time.
2. When students and their parents walk into the library for the pictorial scavenger hunt, you will greet them and then hand them a list of scavenger hunt questions. Encourage participants to ask for help if they are stuck on a question.

Parents are encouraged to accompany students during the scavenger hunt.

3. The librarian should explain that participants must take pictures of their answers rather than write them down.

4. When participants complete the pictorial scavenger hunt, the librarian will check their pictures/answers. The librarian can also give some extra information about the subject of each question, if relevant. Participants who finish the pictorial scavenger hunt will receive a library promotional cup filled with candy of the participant's choice.

ALLERGY WARNINGS

*   Time sensitivity
*   Students may get lost in the library
*   This maybe too much excitement for some students, especially for those who are competitive
*   Candy allergy

CHEF'S NOTES

To add a little extra flavor, include some prizes—stress balls, pens, other library promotional materials, or candy will add to the flavor of this dish. For example, I often reward the participants who complete the pictorial scavenger hunt with our library promotional cup and provide a few varieties of candy with which they can fill their cups. There are no losers in this game; everyone is a winner. If the participants do not have the correct answers, we will help them to find the correct answers.

Twitterbird Cake:
A Tweet-a-licious Scavenger Hunt

Amanda Kraft, Electronic Resources/Reference Librarian, Horry Georgetown Technical College, amanda.kraft@hgtc.edu

NUTRITION INFORMATION

This recipe is designed to help first-year composition and literature students become familiar with resources and services offered at their campus library. The following is a twist on the traditional library scavenger hunt as well as the traditional Southern dessert hummingbird cake.

Students will post photos of the items they discover with a predetermined hashtag in order to better understand the difference between natural language and controlled vocabulary searching.

NUMBERS SERVED

This recipe can be adapted to serve as many students as you can fit into your classroom but has so far been successfully tested on classes with 20 to 25 students broken into three or four groups or, if you will, layers. The number of layers in your cake will be determined by the number of pans (i.e., smartphones/tablets) brought to class.

COOKING TIME

Cooking time depends on how many layers you want your cake to have (i.e., how many groups of students you want) as well as how dense you want your layers to be (i.e., how many items you ask the groups to find). A three- or four-layer cake can take

as little as 30 to 45 minutes, depending on how long it takes to preheat the oven (i.e., provide brief instruction and explain the activity).

ACRL FRAMEWORK ADDRESSED

Information Creation as a Process

MAIN INGREDIENTS

- ☐ 20–25 students
- ☐ 1 professor
- ☐ 1 librarian
- ☐ 3–4 scavenger/hashtag hunts printed (or accessible through LibGuides/ Google docs)
- ☐ 3–4 smartphones
- ☐ 1 classroom with mounted projector
- ☐ 1 library full of books, printers, copiers, scanners, etc.

MAIN COOKING TECHNIQUE

Active learning, group discussion

PREPARATION

- ☐ Create four Twitter accounts for your students to use in case they are uncomfortable using their own accounts or do not have an account. Be sure to type the username and password on the top of the scavenger/hashtag hunts you create.

- ☐ Ask the professor for potential paper topics or content to be covered on the syllabus.
- ☐ Create four scavenger/hashtag hunts (one for each group).
- ☐ Check to make sure that the items you are asking students to find are available, or at least have a plan in place in case these items are checked out in-between classes. For example, you may ask students to discover comparable items on the same or a nearby shelf.
- ☐ Print out, post, and/or share copies of scavenger/hashtag hunts.

COOKING METHOD

1. Preheat the oven: Provide some kind of instruction based on the items you expect the students to discover. A quick demonstration of the library's catalog with tips regarding both natural language (keywords) and controlled vocabulary (subject headings) works well in regard to using hashtags during the hunt.

2. Grease the pan: Ask students with devices to volunteer as group leaders, and help them add their group's account in the Twitter app. If you have devices that the students can borrow, even better.

3. Set the timer: Decide on a time to meet back in the classroom and set

the students loose. Depending on the size of your library, you may choose to offer roving assistance or to make the classroom a home base for questions. Project the live feed of the predetermined hashtag to monitor and share their posts.

4. Stick a fork in it: When everyone returns to the classroom, check out their photos. Talk about their experience and discoveries, and compare the hashtags they used to subject headings.

ALLERGY WARNINGS

Letting your circulation and access staff know when you are planning to whip up this recipe and which ingredients will be used (i.e., which sections of the stacks students will be accessing) is not only courteous but can also lead to a sweeter, much tastier cake, especially if you expect, or even require, students to interact with library staff members other than yourself.

CHEF'S NOTE

This recipe is designed to be delectable but also sets students up for a more sustentative research experience in the future. Encouraging the students to take #shelfies, seeing their smiling faces in the stacks, and retweeting their photos on the library's official feed is the icing on the cake.

ADDITIONAL RESOURCES

Kraft, A. L. & Williams, A. F. (2016). #Shelfies are encouraged: Simple, engaging library instruction with hashtags. *College & Research Libraries News* 77(1): 10–13.

Progressive Three-Course Meal for Library Orientation

Jacalyn Bryan, Associate Professor, Reference & Instructional Services Librarian, Saint Leo University, jacalyn.bryan@saintleo.edu; Elana Karshmer, Associate Professor, Instruction Program & Information Literacy Librarian, Saint Leo University, elana.karshmer@saintleo.edu

NUTRITION INFORMATION

This three-part recipe is integrated into our university's First-Year Experience program and is designed to introduce students to library resources and services. For the "flipped" appetizer, students watch a video introducing them to library space, basic reference services, and resources. The main course is a visit to the library during which students review video topics. For dessert, students complete a graded, written activity using library resources.

NUMBERS SERVED

15–18 students per session

COOKING TIME

- Flipped Appetizer: 15 minutes
- Main Course: 50 minutes
- Dessert: 20–30 minutes

ACRL FRAMEWORK ADDRESSED

- Authority is Constructed and Contextual
- Information Creation as a Process
- Research as Inquiry

MAIN COOKING TECHNIQUE

Flipped classroom, small group cooperative activities, gamification, modeling, discussion

MAIN INGREDIENTS

- ☐ One or two librarian chefs
- ☐ Video and accompanying worksheet
- ☐ Library map activity
- ☐ Self-guided library activity and answer key
- ☐ Computer and TV or projector setup
- ☐ Library Jeopardy (or similar library trivia game)
- ☐ Prizes
- ☐ Library brochures

PREPARATION

- ☐ Schedule library visits
- ☐ Prepare all handouts and worksheets
- ☐ Set up signage for map activity
- ☐ Set up audio/visual equipment
- ☐ Purchase prizes

COOKING METHOD

1. "Flipped" Appetizer: Students watch the library video outside of their "introduction to college" course and complete a worksheet while viewing the video in order to guide them through the content. The students will later bring the worksheet to their scheduled in-library session. The video includes a tour of the library, information about library services, and an introduction to the library catalog and databases. As an alternative to a video, librarians can provide a PowerPoint presentation, brochure, and/or tutorials on the library website that address the pertinent information. To create low-cost videos or presentations, librarians can use tools such as GoAnimate, Smilebox, or Animoto. Students should also be provided with a worksheet to guide them through these materials, which are to be viewed before the library visit.

2. Main Course: Students come to the library with their "introduction to college class" and participate in the library map activity in small groups of three to five. During the activity, students visit specific locations in the library and answer questions about the resources and services that are available; this is a timed activity, which takes approximately 10 minutes and is followed by a review of the correct answers. The librarians then provide a brief demonstration of searching in the library catalog and a subscription database, followed by a discussion of how to evaluate information. The session ends with the Library Jeopardy game, played by students in teams of three to five. This game reviews information from the video and library session in a fun and engaging way, with prizes awarded to the winning team.

The categories for Library Jeopardy could include "Places in the Library," "Library Catalog," and "Databases." The clues are arranged according to Bloom's taxonomy, with higher points awarded for clues that require more complex thinking. If no one answers a clue correctly, the librarians use this as an opportunity to explain the correct answer and any background information necessary to reinforce the concept.

3. Dessert: No more than two weeks after the library session, students complete a library worksheet outside of class as an independent activity. The worksheet requires them to come to the library and to use the library website, catalog, and a subscription database, to locate information and answer questions about key library concepts. This is a graded assignment, and course instructors are provided with an answer key.

ALLERGY WARNINGS

Students should be advised to turn off their cell phones and put them out of sight for the duration of the library session. We have found that students may wander off during the map activity, so it's a good idea to provide time updates every few minutes to keep them on task and, if possible, to station staff or student assistants on different floors of the library to keep them from lingering on landings. To combat attention loss during demonstrations, it's useful to remind students that the review will help them prepare for the Library Jeopardy game.

CHEF'S NOTE

Using a blend of flipped classroom, small group cooperative activities, and gamification provides a meaningful introduction to library services and resources for first-year students. It is important to evaluate this program with the integration of the formative and summative assessments described above. In addition, students have an opportunity to evaluate the in-library session, which provides the librarians with valuable feedback. Our overarching goal for this recipe is to establish a positive connection to the library as students begin their academic studies.

ADDITIONAL RESOURCES

GoAnimate: https://goanimate.com/
Smilebox: http://www.smilebox.com/
Animoto: https://animoto.com

Camera Rolls:
ESOL Student Library Orientation
Joy Oehlers, Information Literacy Librarian, Kapiolani Community College, joy.oehlers@hawaii.edu

NUTRITION INFORMATION
Introduction: Based on information and instructions provided by the librarian and class instructor, English for Speakers of Other Languages (ESOL) students write their own script and use their smartphones to make a two-minute orientation video to teach their classmates how to find, borrow, and renew books. Students enjoy using smartphones or video cameras as media to post information. This fun group activity uses a familiar tool for ESOL students to make sense of their library collections and basic services.

NUMBERS SERVED
20 students: Four groups of five students. Two groups work on the same topic.

COOKING TIME
One hour

DIETARY GUIDELINES
This activity provides opportunities for ESOL students to:
- Speak with staff at library service desks and remove barriers between students and librarians.
- Use the library catalog to locate books and understand how books are organized.
- Practice reading comprehension and public speaking.

- Teach and empower their peers through their videos.

ACRL FRAMEWORK ADDRESSED
- Searching as Strategic Exploration
- Information Creation as a Process

MAIN INGREDIENTS
- ☐ Students bring their smartphones or video cameras, tripods, selfie sticks, and peripheral devices to connect to library computers
- ☐ Librarian and instructors prepare sets of information for each group
- ☐ Tables for group work
- ☐ Props such as mascot, cardboard, markers, etc.
- ☐ Computers with video and image capture apps; for example, Jing

MAIN COOKING TECHNIQUE
Active learning, flipped jigsaw, group participation, storytelling, reflective questioning

PREPARATION
- ☐ Pre-test and post-test (http://bit.ly/1WIUNvO)
- ☐ Instructions and grading rubric for producing videos to:
  - » Find books (http://bit.ly/1WIVaXf)
  - » Borrow and renew books (http://bit.ly/25SPLi3)

- ☐ Summative assessment rubric (http://bit.ly/1Ub1UcO)

COOKING METHOD
1. Librarian will:
   a. Administer pre-test clicker survey.
   b. Introduce the aims of the two activities.
   c. Remind students to read the step-by-step instructions sheets, especially the tips.
   d. Provide examples of what they can do; stress that planning is most important.
   e. Assure students that their videos will not be published. (10 minutes)
2. Students, in their groups, will:
   a. Decide on style and choice of props, if using.
   b. Write script and storyboard.
   c. Shoot video. (30 minutes)
3. Screen videos. (four 2-minute videos)
4. Group reflection questions:
   a. What were some problems your group encountered?
   b. What did your group learn from completing this video?
   c. What did you enjoy most?
   d. Post-test survey. (10 minutes)

ALLERGY WARNINGS

- Students tend to spend more time videoing than planning.
- Some personal equipment may not be compatible with library equipment.
- Time may be needed to sync different user interfaces, smartphones, and projector.

CHEF'S NOTE

Having two groups working on the same topic is not repetitive because each group is likely to present the information in a different way. This contributes to a richer learning experience for their peers.

ADDITIONAL RESOURCES

- Benedict, L., & Pence, H. (2012). "Teaching chemistry using student-created videos and photo blogs accessed with smartphones and two-dimensional barcodes." *Journal of Chemical Education*, 89(4), 492–496.
- Greene, H., & Crespi, C. (2012). "The value of student created videos in the college classroom: An exploratory study in marketing and accounting." *International Journal of Arts and Sciences*, 5(1), 273–283.

Making Zines:
Content Creation with First-year and Transfer Students

Nick Ferreira, Reference and Instruction Librarian, School of the Art Institute of Chicago, nferre1@artic.edu; Mackenzie Salisbury, Reference and Instruction Librarian, School of the Art Institute of Chicago, ssalis1@artic.edu

NUTRITION INFORMATION
Traditional information literacy instruction rarely invites students to become content creators. Utilizing instruction-based art from conceptual artists, such as Yoko Ono and Sol Lewitt, we invite students to approach the library resources as source material, moving beyond the typical research paper. This library project is for students who may have already had an introduction to the library's resources or are transfer students. This can also be used as a scavenger hunt/ introduction to the library.

During this exercise, students will revisit searching the catalog and searching for full-text articles. However, students will not be writing research papers. Instead, they will be using the catalog and article databases to find source material for their blackout collages. This exercise's end product will be a zine, with each student creating one page. Their pages will entail editing texts found in a "blackout poem"—redacted text using a permanent marker.

This recipe came about after working with faculty who teach the first-year class with transfer students. We realized that many students already understood the basic concepts of research in a college library. What students needed was a quick refresher on college-level research and practical knowledge of their new library's logistics. This exercise allows students to actively search article databases and the library catalog as well as physically locate items on the shelf. They also will find out where other high-use resources are, such as photocopiers, scanners, and printers.

NUMBERS SERVED
15–20 students

COOKING TIME
90–120 minutes

DIETARY GUIDELINES
Through these nontraditional research methods, we encourage students to browse and embrace serendipity in research and open a dialog about becoming information contributors themselves. This exercise also begins conversations around authorship, appropriation, and the library as a source of inspiration.

ACRL FRAMEWORKS ADDRESSED
- Searching as Strategic Exploration
- Information Has Value
- Scholarship as Conversation

MAIN INGREDIENTS
- ☐ Physical collection
- ☐ Database with fulltext/PDF articles
- ☐ Black markers
- ☐ Printer
- ☐ Photocopier
- ☐ Glue
- ☐ Half-letter-size paper template

MAIN COOKING TECHNIQUE
Active learning, art making

COOKING METHOD
Remix Project, Student Instructions:
1. You will work with a partner on this project.
2. Find a piece of writing that pertains to the remix project you have been working on.
3. One of you will find a book and one of you will find a journal article.
4. Print or photocopy your one page from either your book or journal article. Scale each of your selections to fit on one half of the 8.5"x11" piece of paper provided.
5. Use black markers to block out portions of your partner's selection.
6. Glue your edited partner's text to the paper provided (it has a line on it, so pick a side).

7. Photocopy the page with both of your edited selections.
8. Give this to your instructor.

ALLERGY WARNINGS

Either make front and back covers yourself or have students who finish early make them on the half-letter template pages. This will add 2 pages to your final count. Make sure the final number of pages is divisible by 4. In other words, if you have 13 students and you include the 2 pages for front and back cover, you'll need to make 1 more page. You could make a list of students who participated, a brief introduction, or leave it blank; it's entirely up to you. Take your pages and photocopy them double-sided. The only page where order matters is the cover, or if you had to add a list of participants or blank pages. We would recommend adding them on the inside back covers.

CHEF'S NOTE

Students will be "remixing" their partner's selection during this exercise. It would be appropriate (pun intended) to have discussions regarding sources, remix, and appropriation. Artists and writers, such as William S. Burroughs, Penelope Umbrico, and Austin Kleon, who have used remix and appropriation, are good examples to show during the class session.

Cognition Connection:
Student Mapping of the Library Experience

Marissa Mourer, Arts, Humanities, and Social Sciences Librarian, Humboldt State University, marissa@humboldt.edu

NUTRITION INFORMATION
This recipe utilizes cognitive, hands-on mapping. Students create maps based on what they recall following a library tour within a one-shot instructional or orientation session. Mapping creatively engages students' own recollections and further commits their experience to memory.

NUMBERS SERVED
Serves no more than 50 students

COOKING TIME
30 to 90 minutes, depending on your library size

DIETARY GUIDELINES
This recipe is designed to engage students using a hands-on activity following a traditional library tour.

ACRL FRAMEWORKS ADDRESSED
Information Creation as a Process

MAIN INGREDIENTS
☐ Structured library tour. Address the whole library environment. Include library resources, services, and amenities, such as technology, artwork, and furniture. Aim to note what generally goes unspoken.

☐ Printed library floor maps. Print maps large enough to fill-in, but condense number of printed pages. I print two floors per page and double-sided. Students generally prioritize drawing infrastructure, so provide this for them. Edit an existing library infrastructure map to digitally erase all details; I use Adobe Acrobat. I add a compass and note the instructional classroom or lobby as a point of reference.

☐ Two different-colored ink pens for each student. Avoid blue or black.

MAIN COOKING TECHNIQUE
Library tour, written mapping activity, and group reflection

PREPARATION
Expect questions. As you acknowledge student usage of the library or artwork, students may ask many questions during the tour. Have blank maps and pens ready to use immediately following the tour. I have had success providing basic library catalog searching instruction before the tour.

COOKING METHOD
1. Inform students that they will be participating in a tour and mapping activity, which requires their attention throughout.

2. Lead library tour. Fifteen minutes is effective for small libraries. Return to instructional space.

3. Inform students that mapping assists in interpreting spaces and committing new information to memory. Inform students that you will collect maps and share with their instructor.

4. Instruct students that this is an incredibly short, timed activity. They should write notes quickly about anything they recall. Remind students to write on all printed maps. Encourage questions prior to starting the activity.

5. Pass out printed maps and the ink pens to each student.

6. On your cue, tell students to pick up the same ink color pen (e.g., green) and note their memories on the maps. Time this activity and firmly end at 1.5–2 minutes.

7. On your cue, have students pick up the other pen (e.g., red) and continue making notes for another 1.5–2 minutes.

8. Observe students throughout both rounds. Continue with a third round if notetaking is especially active; students can use their own pen/pencil. Collect materials.

9. Debrief as a group.
   a. Explain that students used different ink to capture the order of their recollections, and that you use their

maps to shape future library tours and instruction.

b. Invite a few students to share something that stood out to them on the tour and why, or within small groups if time permits. Inform students that this discussion further encourages recollection.

ALLERGY WARNINGS

- Students with disabilities should be accommodated. Ask instructors to insure inclusion, e.g., use an elevator with a student if the entire class cannot use. Be mindful of phrases like "walk this way" or "see this." Computers or blank sheets can be used for mapping; just instruct students to organize notes by floor. Additional time can also be given.
- Decide on key places to stop and share helpful details instead of talking throughout the tour. Students may initially balk at taking a tour. If you notice that attention wanes at particular places, try noting something peculiar or witty about that space/resource; I often find these noted verbatim on maps.

CHEF'S NOTE

Cognitive mapping can be a great way to bring active learning to a passive tour strategy. Maps are tangible assessments about the purpose and impact of a tour. Students have responded favorably to the creative opportunity. Expect maps full of doodles as well as enthusiastic notes or questions that

can be addressed during the debrief. I also use maps to see where students may have lost attention and easily modify my next tour. Although few instructors might express interest in reviewing the maps, maps can serve to start conversations with faculty in addition to students.

ADDITIONAL RESOURCES

To learn more about cognitive mapping, you can read my short reflection piece and a bibliography here: http://acrl.ala.org/IS/cognitive-mapping-the-library-tour/

This instructional activity was adapted from the cognitive mapping research methodology used in College Libraries and Student Culture: What We Now Know. (2012). Chicago: American Library Association.

Cooking up the Cephalonian Method for Honors Orientation

Brenda Yates Habich, Information Services Librarian, Ball State University, bhabich@bsu.edu

NUTRITION INFORMATION

The Cephalonian Method, an active learning method, allows for the librarian to focus on content and collections that are most important to new students on physical tours of the library. Librarians construct questions ahead of time that students will ask to learn what the library has for them.

This recipe was created to address the need for incoming Honors College students to experience an orientation to their academic library. It supports the Honors College Peer Mentors Program. New Honors students are required to take a 1-credit hour, 8-week course that is taught by an upper-classman in the Honors College. These mentors apply through the Honors College and work with the Director of the Peer Mentors Program, are paid, and will often team-teach with another Honors mentor. The Honors 100 course is designed to help new Honors students acclimate to the college campus. The course covers a variety of topics, and the library session is required for passing the class.

NUMBERS SERVED

8 to 16 in each session (total number of sessions can be as many as 40+)

COOKING TIME

Between 50 and 75 minutes—very flexible, depending on how well done you prefer your orientation. Recipe can be modified according to time, size of group, focus of collections, etc.

DIETARY GUIDELINES

The overall purpose of this recipe is to familiarize students with an academic library and what it can offer them during their undergraduate experience and to introduce information literacy concepts to new Honors College students. These sessions are a foundation for the Framework for Information Literacy and can be used as a starting point for future research instruction experiences and discussions about Information Literacy.

This recipe can be modified to accommodate other groups that request a physical tour. For example, Summer Bridge, 21st Century Scholars, Dual Credit, and others can benefit from knowing about information literacy and library resources.

MAIN INGREDIENTS

- ☐ Group of students (7–14 /session works best)
- ☐ Ideas/questions about the physical library that you want to highlight

- ☐ A set of questions and answers that will be used for each floor/area of the library (an answer sheet for the librarian to use when answering and discussing the questions)
- ☐ Questions on color-coded index cards for students
- ☐ Classroom with an instructor station to briefly demonstrate important online resources
- ☐ LibCal or another online registration system
- ☐ Schedule of classes with mentors assigned

MAIN COOKING TECHNIQUE

Active learning, tour

PREPARATION

- ☐ Before the Honors groups attend their library session, set up a calendar using LibCal or other online calendar system. (The Honors 100 class schedule is shared by the Director of the Peer Mentor Program with the librarian.)
- ☐ Choose two different dates and times throughout the 8-week course and put them on the calendar for the mentors to choose from (they will only choose one).
- ☐ Once the calendar has been organized, send an email to the student mentors

over the summer, introducing yourself as the librarian. Include what the session will cover, and explain the registration process by providing the link to the calendar for them to pick one date and time. If the times offered do not work, have them contact the librarian directly for scheduling. Encourage mentors to partner with each other for the session.

☐ Keep track of who registers and send email reminders to those who don't schedule.

COOKING METHOD

The Cephalonian Method from Cardiff University in the United Kingdom is used for the physical tour of the library. It is possible to focus on the library's website and direct the questions around useful resources in addition to or separate from the physical tour. If you are working with multiple groups, see the Preparation step for details.

1. Decide what the focus of each floor/area of the library should be.
2. Prepare questions on color-coded index cards representing each floor or area.
3. Give one card per student. All students may not get a card, depending on what the librarian is highlighting and how many questions they have developed.
4. As you do the physical tour/discussion, use the appropriate color card for the floor/area and have students ask the questions on the cards. This allows you call for a "pink card" (see Additional Resources for examples) since you won't know the student by name. Discuss the answer(s) with the students. This method is adjustable to the group size, time, and emphasis needed by the group.
5. After the physical tour, and if time allows, conduct a brief classroom session focusing on website basics.

ALLERGY WARNINGS

It's best to do this session early in the semester when it can be of the most benefit to the new student.

CHEF'S NOTE

The mentors I work with love this activity and stress how important it is for new students to know the information and what the library has for them. I have also found that the flexibility of this recipe is good for changes that the academic library experiences and works as a way to update students of the changes each fall.

ADDITIONAL RESOURCES

Information about the Cephalonian Method: http://www.cardiff.ac.uk/insrv/educationandtraining/infolit/cephalonianmethod/index.html

---

Sample tour questions with locations and card color:

☐ My project focuses on _____. Does the library have any resources that might help me? (second floor, yellow card)

☐ My group needs to print a poster. How do I do that? (second floor, yellow card)

☐ I see a sign that says, "General Collection." What is that? (second floor, yellow card)

☐ How do I print in color? (second floor, yellow card)

☐ How do I get a book that I requested through Interlibrary Loan? (first floor, pink card)

☐ I'm not finding the resources I need for my paper. What do I do? (first floor, pink card)

☐ Where can I find actual newspapers and magazines? (first floor, pink card)

☐ I'd like to have some 3D visuals to add value to my presentation. Does the library have anything that I might be able to use? (lower level, blue card)

☐ I like music. What does the library have that I can check out? (lower level, blue card)

☐ I need to watch a movie for class. How can I do that? (lower level, blue card)

☐ I like to edit videos. Where can I go to do that? (lower level, blue card)

☐ I'm having trouble understanding a concept in class. What Library resources are there to help me? (lower level, blue card)

☐ My laptop crashed. What can I do? (lower level, blue card)

In the Test Kitchen with International Students:
Decoding Research Terminology, Concepts, and Tools

Kelly Cannon, Outreach and Scholarly Communication Librarian, Muhlenberg College, kellycannon@muhlenberg.edu;
Rachel Hamelers, Head of Public Outreach and Information Services, Muhlenberg College, rachelhamelers@muhlenberg.edu;
Jennifer Jarson, Information Literacy and Assessment Librarian, Muhlenberg College, jenniferjarson@muhlenberg.edu

NUTRITION INFORMATION

This recipe was designed to help introduce incoming international students to foundational research skills and concepts during a pre-orientation program. First-year international students often face additional disconnects due to language barriers and different cultural approaches and expectations to academic research and secondary education. Many librarians are asked to give tours during first-year student orientation. It's been our experience, however, that many international students could benefit from orientation to research terminology, concepts, and tools in addition to space and resources.

In this activity, we gave students sample citations and a sample research assignment to simulate what students will encounter on syllabi and in classes in the first days and weeks of the semester. Adapt this recipe so that your international students feel less overwhelmed on the first day of class. After this session they will have steps to follow to tackle their first assignments and projects.

NUMBERS SERVED

We suggest a ratio of at least one instructor per 10–12 students to provide adequate support.

COOKING TIME

Prep time is one hour or less. Cooking time is approximately one hour.

DIETARY GUIDELINES

The larger purpose of this session is to familiarize international students with foundational terminology, concepts, and tools commonly used in research assignments.

ACRL FRAMEWORKS ADDRESSED

- Authority is Constructed and Contextual
- Information Has Value
- Searching as Strategic Exploration

MAIN INGREDIENTS

- ☐ Computer and internet access for all students and instructors
- ☐ Projector and screen
- ☐ Library and librarians' contact information on a sticker or handout

MAIN COOKING TECHNIQUE

Active learning

PREPARATION

Make adjustments to the template below, which consists of our sample citations and assignment, or design your own to better fit your institutional oven. Divide up presenting/facilitating responsibilities among instructors.

MAIN COOKING METHOD

1. Introductions
   a. Begin with a short introduction of instructors. Identify the disciplinary responsibilities of each librarian, making plain to students whom they can contact for help in which subject area (i.e., department/course).
   b. Explain that the purpose of this session is to help prepare students to understand the research language and expectations on syllabi and assignments and become acquainted with key research tools and services. After the session, students will have tools to approach assignments in the first days and weeks of the semester.
2. Parsing and finding citations for assigned readings on a syllabus
   a. Display a sample citation for a journal article on the screen (Figure 1). Pull apart and identify each of the citation's elements: author, publication date, article title, journal title, etc. Model for students how to use the online catalog or discovery tool to locate the full text of the citation.

> **FIGURE 1.** SAMPLE CITATIONS
> Fogarty, R. S. (2003, Spring). In Search of Memory. *Antioch Review*. p. 197.
> Toussaint-Samat, M. (1993). *A History of Food*. Cambridge, MA: Blackwell Reference.

b. Repeat with a sample citation for a book (Figure 1).

c. Give students another sample citation for them to practice finding a source using the online catalog or discovery service.

d. Explain and demonstrate that citations may appear in a syllabus as assigned readings. Students may need to find the cited materials themselves using library resources, including course reserves and interlibrary loan.

3. Decoding an assignment

a. Show students key elements of the library website, such as subject and other research guides and citation guides.

b. Show students a sample assignment (Figure 2). Point out to students the places in the assignment where expectations regarding sources and citation styles are located.

c. Give students another sample assignment. Ask students to respond to the questions in pairs. Have instructors circulate to assist students. Regroup to discuss students' work and address misconceptions or questions.

4. General guiding questions for decoding assignments

a. Highlight the questions in Figure 3 as guides that students can use each time they are given an assignment. This method will help them decode their own assignments and clarify professors' expectations.

b. Give students a handout with these questions as well as librarian contact information for their future use. Encourage students to contact librarians for research assistance.

5. Following up

a. Survey students later in the semester to assess what was helpful to them and what they wished the session had covered to inform future iterations of this activity.

b. Respond to any ongoing concerns or research needs.

FIGURE 2. SAMPLE ASSIGNMENT

Assignment:

After reading James Joyce's *Finnegan's Wake*, write a one-page essay on a theme you see in this book that you also saw when we read *Ulysses*. Use at least two examples from each text. Your one-page paper is due on October 3rd.

The next phase of the assignment is to find at least two scholarly literary criticisms on *Finnegan's Wake*. Integrate them into what you wrote in the original one-page essay, constructing a second essay. This second essay should be no more than five pages double spaced. Use the MLA citation format. The second essay is due November 1st.

If you do not have your own copy, there is a copy of *Finnegan's Wake* on reserve at the library.

Questions:

• What kind of sources does this assignment require you to use?

• Which subject guide on the library website would you use to find sources for this assignment? Find at least two of these sources using the library website.

• Which citation style would you use? Where on the library website is there a guide to help with this citation style? What other sources exist to help with citations?

• What resources are available to you for help with research?

FIGURE 3. GUIDING QUESTIONS FOR DECODING RESEARCH ASSIGNMENTS

- Which discipline? (So that students know which subject guide to use or which librarian to ask for research assistance.)

- What kind of sources (e.g., scholarly, popular, primary, secondary) do you need?

- Which citation style should you use?

- Where would you find these types of sources?

ALLERGY WARNINGS

- We suggest breaking students up into smaller groups, possibly by language skill. That way, you can pace the sessions more appropriately.
- Reduce time devoted to lecture as much as possible. Hands-on practice for students is the most important part of the session.
- Consider making an outline of the session for students to help them follow along and take notes for their future reference.

CHEF'S NOTE

Although we do not think that a library tour alone is enough preparation for international students, we do think it provides a nice appetizer to the main course. Students like to see the library space, and often have questions about what the library offers.

PART II. LIBRARY INSTRUCTION
General FYE and First Year Discipline-Based Instruction

Bite-Sized Wikipedia Editing Assignment

Lindsay McNiff, Learning and Instruction Librarian, Dalhousie University, lindsay.mcniff@dal.ca

NUTRITION INFORMATION

In a summer program for academically dismissed students, participants complete a short research assignment that involves updating a Wikipedia page by adding either a missing citation or new (cited) information.

NUMBERS SERVED

Serves 10–15 students, but can easily be adapted

COOKING TIME

90 minutes

DIETARY GUIDELINES

- The goals are to get students using and evaluating information sources beyond Wikipedia in order to improve Wikipedia, to tie research to accountability beyond the classroom, and to make Wikipedia editing work in a one-shot. This assignment can tie in with many different instruction sessions and is a great way to introduce first-year students to the benefits and drawbacks of Wikipedia.
- This activity provides many opportunities for students to think critically about information.

ACRL FRAMEWORK ADDRESSED

- Information Has Value
- Authority is Constructed and Contextual

MAIN INGREDIENTS

- ☐ Help documentation for editing Wikipedia (handout or video)
- ☐ Internet connection

MAIN COOKING TECHNIQUE

Lecture and discussion, hands-on practice (if computers are available), take-home assignment

PREPARATION

- ☐ Create help documentation for editing Wikipedia
- ☐ Supply students with a list of potential topics (optional)
- ☐ Create assignment (outlined below)

COOKING METHOD

This assignment has four basic components whose flavours can be adjusted depending on taste preferences:

1. Select a topic: Students must choose a topic for which the Wikipedia page needs additional citations. Students can choose from a list provided by the instructor, or can search for a topic using the following search: *site: en.wikipedia. org "needs additional citations" keywords*. Students save the "before" version of the page as a PDF.
2. Research the topic: Students are required to find three sources (scholarly books or articles) on the topic and write

brief annotations analyzing the value of each source using criteria discussed in the session.

3. Edit Wikipedia: Using the provided instructional material, students edit Wikipedia by either adding a citation or adding a new piece of information and a citation. Students save the "after" version of the page as a PDF.
4. Reflect: Students write a short paragraph reflecting on this experience. Prompt questions might include: *Has your view of Wikipedia changed? Do you feel more confident as a researcher?*

ALLERGY WARNINGS

- As always, students are more likely to embrace library assignments when grades are a factor. Work with the professor or program coordinator to make sure the grades are added to the mix.
- Wikipedia citations might look different from the types of citations students are accustomed to. Making this distinction before students start on the assignment may be helpful.
- Ideally, this should be a take-home assignment so students have an opportunity to reflect on their sources and on the process, and to ensure their Wikipedia contributions are not rushed and underdone.

- With the technicalities of editing Wikipedia, the important source evaluation piece of this assignment has the potential to be overlooked. Try to use instruction time wisely to discuss source evaluation, authority, and context with students.

CHEF'S NOTE

- This assignment is designed to facilitate discovery, and the reflection section is always illuminating. Students are amazed to realize how easy it is to edit Wikipedia (which they often claim to have known, but not *known*), and their thoughts on Wikipedia as an information tool become more nuanced and informed.
- When students feel that their work has value within a larger body of knowledge, their sense of responsibility is strengthened. This can be a key understanding for any first-year student, but might have particular meaning for at-risk groups.
- This assignment can provide good context for those dreaded one-shot sessions that are not tied to assignments and might otherwise seem nebulous to students.

Ruminating on Metadata:
Deconstructed Database with Twitter Feed and Fluid Comparison

Jessica Denke, Public Services Librarian, DeSales University, Jessica.Denke@desales.edu

NUTRITION INFORMATION

This appetizer relates Twitter hashtags and familiar metadata to database metadata and controlled language. Students are then introduced to strategic searching through utilization of subject searches and other variables, such as publisher, publication, industry, geography, etc. within a database.

COOKING TIME

Cooking time for this appetizer is approximately 30 minutes and can be themed to a specific class, assignment, or popular news event. Cooking time can be altered depending upon included dietary frames; see Allergy Warnings.

ACRL FRAMEWORK ADDRESSED

- Scholarship as Conversation
- Information Creation as a Process
- Searching as Strategic Exploration

MAIN COOKING TECHNIQUE

Lively discussion during the instruction session, brainstorming, hands on experience

MAIN INGREDIENTS

☐ Internet access
☐ Instructor's workstation
☐ Student workstations
☐ Millennials

PREPARATION

Select a trending Twitter hashtag feed that has some relevance to the class, whether it be related to an assignment or discipline-related news event. A feed is most effective if participants can be seen directly engaging one another and if one or more participants have subject authority or first-person experience.

THE INSTRUCTION SESSION

1. Librarian brings up the pre-selected Twitter conversation for the class to see. Students are encouraged to locate a feed if they have a Twitter account.
2. Librarian presents a trending Twitter conversation found through the identified hashtag. Individuals involved in conversation are introduced.
3. Librarian identifies metadata as data that describes other data, utilizing the identified hashtag as an example.
4. Students are asked to identify additional metadata related to particular Twitter postings. Examples include: date/time, number of engagements (retweets and likes), and other hashtags.
5. Librarian explains that hashtags in Twitter are very similar to the controlled language of a database, which is manipulated through subject searching. Librarian relates Twitter post metadata to the metadata of an academic journal article within a database. Direct comparisons are made between hashtags and subject searching and post metadata and other variables used within the database to refine retrieved results.
6. Students are given 15 minutes to implement their knowledge of metadata to strategically search a library database and obtain an article to support an upcoming assignment.

ALLERGY WARNINGS

Trending Twitter conversations are dynamic and spoil quickly when exposed; quality is hard to guarantee. This environment provides ample opportunity to discuss critical evaluation of contributions and how information is valued differently depending on context. If time allows, the information creation as a process frame may be addressed.

CHEF'S NOTE

Students enjoy the familiarity of this activity, and understanding metadata demystifies the process of researching in library databases.

A Melting Pot of Fondue:
Embedding a Librarian into a FYE Course

Kyrille Goldbeck DeBose, College Librarian for Natural Resources & Environment and Animal Sciences, Coordinator of Instruction and Research Projects for the Vet Med Library, Virginia Tech, kdebose@vt.edu

NUTRITION INFORMATION

This set of lesson plans was originally designed for a freshman First-Year Experience (FYE) course in the College of Natural Resources and Environment, but the examples used can be adjusted to other disciplines as needed. It is comprised of three distinct sessions (servings) with specific learning objectives and activities to guide students through the literature review and research process. Each serving includes a set of online videos and corresponding quiz which are to be completed before the in-class presentation and corresponding activities are delivered.

Learning outcomes for serving 1:

- Explain the general process to conduct a literature review about a topic.
- Select a topic of interest to research that follows course guidelines.
- Identify current self-knowledge and gaps of self-knowledge about the topic.
- Examine background sources to develop a knowledge base regarding the topic.
- Create research questions and refine the research topic.
- Identify synonyms and additional concepts to use as keywords.

Learning outcomes for serving 2:

- Identify specific characteristics of a variety of information sources in order to locate appropriate and credible information sources for the project.
- Describe how the information timeline influences what types of information sources are available for a topic.
- Construct a search statement using Boolean operators appropriately.
- Select relevant databases to search about the topic.
- Demonstrate how to access information sources found through the library's databases and discovery search engine.

Learning outcomes for serving 3:

- Apply evaluation criteria to select appropriate information sources for the project.
- Discuss the importance of properly citing sources.
- Demonstrate how to find an information source using a citation.
- Identify the necessary components to construct a citation for different types of information sources.
- Illustrate how to cite a source using the assigned citation style.
- Construct an annotated bibliography for each cited item used in the literature review.

NUMBERS SERVED

80–100, but can be scaled as needed

COOKING TIME

- Three 50-minute in-person sessions
- Three online modules (< 30 minutes each)
- Four worksheets to be completed outside of class

DIETARY GUIDELINES

The purpose of this recipe is to expose students to the skills necessary for conducting literature reviews as a part of the research process, along with developing critical thinking skills, ability to synthesize content, and create new scholarly products.

ACRL FRAMEWORK ADDRESSED

The information literacy skills that are addressed through the online videos, lecture content, and activities directly correspond to all six attributes outlined in ACRL's Framework (http://www.ala.org/acrl/standards/ilframework). The focus is on "Research as Inquiry," but each area is covered at an introductory level. This approach was used to familiarize students with several concepts across the framework and create a foundational knowledge base to be built upon throughout their academic careers.

MAIN INGREDIENTS

- ☐ Pre-class videos and quiz for each serving (described in the "Preparation" section)
- ☐ A classroom with a computer and projector to display presentation slides
- ☐ Presentation slides with content that addresses the learning outcomes for each serving (described in the "Cooking Method" section)
- ☐ Corresponding worksheets for each serving (described in the "Cooking Method" section)

MAIN COOKING TECHNIQUE

Flipped classroom, in-person lecture with discussions, and worksheets

PREPARATION

Prior to each in-class presentation, students are required to watch three videos (available through YouTube) and take a corresponding 5-point online quiz. Quizzes are a mix of multiple choice and true/false questions. Several questions per video are incorporated into a randomized question pool, designed so at least one question from each video is included as a part of each serving's quiz. Students are granted two attempts to complete the quiz, but they may not see the same questions. The highest quiz score is recorded. Answers to commonly missed questions are addressed during the corresponding in-class presentations for each serving.
Note: It is best if these quizzes can be administered and automatically graded through a Learning/Course Management System.

Serving 1 pre-class work:

- Developing your topic (https://www.youtube.com/watch?v=x4XZxIqSuyY) (2:42) by UNC-Chapel Hill
- Building your knowledge base (https://www.youtube.com/watch?v=15f0r2fi0y8) (3:34) by UNC-Chapel Hill
- Recognizing the potential in your search results (https://www.youtube.com/watch?v=57TSI69l9Qs)(3:02) by UNC-Chapel Hill

Serving 2 pre-class work:

- The information cycle (https://www.youtube.com/watch?v=drej6K44avl) (4:49) by UW-Oshkosh Polk Library
- Popular vs. Scholarly sources (https://www.youtube.com/watch?v=Qlw6PuR8oBk)(4:03) by Hartness Library
- Basics of Boolean operators (https://www.youtube.com/watch?v=4qKDQKJCp-s)(2:14) by Douglas College

Serving 3 pre-class work:

- Me? Plagiarize? (https://www.youtube.com/watch?v=TdMg7Yu4mPs)(3:39) by Hartness Library
- Using sources (https://www.youtube.com/watch?v=6_O6m4FDkxQ)(4:56) by Hartness Library
- Why we cite (https://www.youtube.com/watch?v=mkn4SyhjyIM)(2:30) by University of North Carolina

COOKING METHOD

The following steps are employed for each of the servings, with the corresponding content and worksheets assigned as noted:

- Step 1: Create slides that incorporate the learning outcomes for each serving, with holding places for student responses to the online quizzes. Use the same example research topic across all three servings. Include screenshots of filled-out worksheets for each corresponding serving, so students see how the content of the slides and in-class demonstrations fit in with the expectations of the worksheets they are to complete.
- Step 2: Provide students with a link to (or embed in an online learning management system) the three videos and quiz associated for the corresponding serving. The due date for completion of the quiz should be (at a minimum) the day before the librarian-led in-class presentation is given.
- Step 3: Incorporate quiz responses of the most incorrectly answered questions into the slide presentation for discussion during the in-class session.
- Step 4: Give the in-class presentations for each serving, incorporate the learning outcomes relating to:
  - » Serving 1:
    - – Topic selection; using background resources; refining the topic; developing specific research questions to be addressed; identifying appropriate keywords

» Serving 2:
- Recognizing different types of information sources; selecting appropriate resources (e.g. databases, search engines) to search; developing effective search statements; accessing desired information sources

» Serving 3:
- Locating information sources from a bibliography; evaluating sources; creating an annotated bibliography; citing sources using the assigned citation style for the course

- Step 5: Assign corresponding worksheets for each serving:
  » Serving 1:
  - "What do I want to know?"
    ○ Acknowledges current self-knowledge, detects gaps in self-knowledgebase, and identifies areas to explore about the topic.
  - "Concept Table"
    ○ Walks students through developing research questions and creating keywords for their concepts.
  » Serving 2:
  - "Building Search Strategies & Research log"
    ○ Shows students how to use the "Search Strategy Builder" (http://www.lib.vt.edu/help/portal/search-strategy-builder.html) to copy and paste searches into library databases.

■ Search Strategy Builder was created by University of Arizona Libraries and is licensed under a Creative Commons Attribution-NonCommercial-ShareAlike 3.0 Unported License.
  ○ Shows students how to keep track of what was searched and what databases provided the most useful results about their topic.
  » Serving 3:
  - "Evaluating sources"
    ○ Provides a list of the seven evaluation criteria that students are to use to analyze each source initially selected about the topic.
    ○ Students are to integrate their evaluation criteria as part of their annotated bibliographies in order to justify the sources ultimately chosen for the research project.
- Step 6: Be available after the librarian-led sessions have concluded to assist students with any questions they may have about the research project (e.g. identifying appropriate databases, assist with search strategies, provide feedback regarding the assigned citation style, etc.).

ALLERGY WARNINGS
This is a time-intensive embedded experience as it includes: continually updating content, identifying alternative videos, refining quiz questions, meeting weekly with course instructors, analyzing and incorporating quiz responses into lectures, and consulting with students that request additional assistance outside of class.

CHEF'S NOTE
Demonstrating with a research topic that ties in with another related activity the students will do later in the course is extremely helpful. In this course, the research topic ultimately chosen as the demonstration topic was about white-tailed deer. This was selected because the exercises in a lab session midway through the semester require students to read a short article on white-tailed deer management and then build a conceptual map as a practice activity for what they will turn in regarding their own research projects. Having been exposed to different research aspects about white-tailed deer during the library instruction sessions, students were better able to connect the conceptual model exercise to the information and skills they obtained during the library instruction sessions.

ADDITIONAL RESOURCES
University of Arizona. (2009). Search Strategy Builder. http://www.library.arizona.edu/applications/quickHelp/tutorials/view_information/152/page:6 [Last accessed: June 6, 2016]

ATTACHMENTS
- Concept Table Worksheet
- Evaluating Sources Worksheet

INFORMATION RESEARCH
Developing your topic

1. Choose a research idea. Refine it into a clear, one sentence statement of what you will be investigating. Write a list of questions that you need your research to answer.
   a. Research statement (thesis/topic statement, research question):
   b. Research Questions:
      i.

      ii.

      iii.

2. Identify the essential concepts (ideas) in your research statement and complete the Concept Table below. Enter your essential concepts (nouns) in the Concept Categories cells—the most important concept is the Primary one. Secondary concepts modify or tell you something about the Primary concept. Enter synonyms for each concept in the column below that concept term.

CONCEPT TABLE

Concept Categories	Primary Concept	Secondary Concepts			
		1	2	3	4
Synonyms					

kgd 9-14

RELIABILITY EVALUATION CHECKLIST

Evaluating resource reliability
Evaluation criteria
Usefulness/Relevance/Coverage
Contains detailed information one specific aspect of your topic
Contains a clear overview of your topic
What part of this resource did you find addresses your topic that you will most likely use/cite in your paper or presentation?
Authority/Authorship
Author(s) are clearly identified
Credentials of the author(s) are identified
Author'(s) credentials are appropriate for the subject
Type of source is easily determined (e.g. website, blog, scholarly article, news article, etc)
Accuracy
Author(s) are recognized expert(s) on the subject
Information is well-organize and well-written (no typos/errors)
Information is clearly documented and sources are cited
Sources cited are generally recognized as reliable

Objectivity
Source explicitly states its purpose and/or audience
Information addresses multiple points of view on the topic
A variety of reliable sources are cited
Currency
Publication or copyright date is given
The publication date is appropriate to your information need
Audience
Intended audience is easy to identify
Intended audience is scholarly, professional, or knowledgeable about the topic
Logical Fallacies
No logical fallacies can be found in the text
Presents logical conclusions supported by documentation

Spoiling Their Dinner:
Using Candy to Incentivize Active Learning for Multiple Learning Styles

Rebecca Johnson, Instruction & Emerging Technologies Librarian, Manchester University, rejohnson@manchester.edu; Edita Sicken, Instruction & Access Services Librarian, Manchester University, epsicken@manchester.edu

NUTRITION INFORMATION

This recipe is designed to give first-year students an opportunity to engage in purposeful learning about library resources and research. In this student-led session, the entire research process—from brainstorming topics and keywords to evaluating resources—will be covered.

The instructional template outlined below is easily adaptable for all First-Year Experience course sections—just switch out the topic! Doing so allows you to establish a consistent research foundation for all first-year students without having to worry about creating dozens (or more!) unique lesson plans.

NUMBERS SERVED
10–20 students

COOKING TIME
50–75 minutes

DIETARY GUIDELINES
The purpose of this recipe is to get students engaged in the one-shot session instead of passively receiving the information. Kolb's Experiential Learning Theory is used to cycle students through four stages of learning that includes experimentation, experience, reflection, and conceptualization. In this model of instruction, reflection is key as it gives students the opportunity to process and critically think about information sought and found.

Building the session with Kolb's model in mind, as well as ACRL's overarching Framework for Information Literacy, allows us to diversify learning in such a way that all types of student learners have the chance to attain the same information in a meaningful and relevant way. Not only that, but Kolb's model incorporates peer learning which adds a layer of critical thinking that is foundational to the Framework for Information Literacy.

ACRL FRAMEWORK ADDRESSED
- Research as Inquiry
- Searching as Strategic Exploration

MAIN INGREDIENTS
- ☐ Active learning worksheet (See Figure 1)
- ☐ Notecards
- ☐ Computer lab
- ☐ Research assignment/topic
- ☐ Sample research topics
- ☐ Google Forms
- ☐ Candy!

MAIN COOKING TECHNIQUE
Active listening and learning, group discussion, and individual reflection

PREPARATION
- ☐ Course research guide (optional). Prepare a research guide with relevant library resources for the assignment and search strategy tips.
- ☐ Design session around Kolb's learning cycle (See Figure 2). Create a cycle of instruction activities with each segment corresponding to one specific aspect of Kolb's model, giving students the opportunity to learn through concrete experiences, reflective observations, abstract conceptualization, and active experimentation.
- ☐ Design an active learning worksheet for students to use when completing session activities. (See Figure 1)
- ☐ Google Form intro questionnaire. Prepare a survey to be given to students prior to the research session. This survey should ask students to reflect upon their previous research experiences and their knowledge of the research assignment.

FYS: Diseases & Their Effects on Humans
Rebecca Johnson & Edita Sicken | http://libguides.manchester.edu/FYSpolando

Research Essay

Name of Disease:

Keywords

Synonyms Found:	Aspects of Disease Found:

Resources (Databases) Used:

Notes

Have Questions? Book An Appointment

FIGURE 1. ACTIVE LEARNING WORKSHEET EXAMPLE

COOKING METHOD

1. Prior to class
   a. The librarian should send students the prepared introductory Google Form at least a day prior to the instruction session.
   b. On the day of the session, assess the answers to gauge student familiarity with their assignment and the research process.
2. Introduction
   a. Prior to the start of the session, pass out one notecard and one active learning worksheet per student. Additionally, have the Google Form questionnaire on the screen for students who have not yet completed it.
   b. If possible, corral students into easily grouped seating arrangements. No stragglers!
   c. Once the session begins, go over standard introductory information such as: introducing one's self, how to contact a librarian, and what the session will cover.
3. Active Lecture—Path to Resources *[Active Experimentation]*
   a. Have students take on an instructional role to lead their peers to the course guides—specifically to the one for their First-Year Experience course.
   b. Offer the first round of candy to the student who volunteers to guide the rest of the class to their course guide.
   c. Quickly cover the resources found in the course guide and where to locate contact information for further assistance outside of class.
4. Topic Development *[Concrete Experience and Reflective Observation]*
   a. Students work in groups while using the active learning worksheet to reflect on the assignment topic and generate research questions.
   b. From the topics shared by the groups, choose one topic to pursue for the remainder of the session.
   c. Working in the same groups, students brainstorm keywords and synonyms for the topic and perform preliminary searches in a general database to develop familiarity with subject headings.

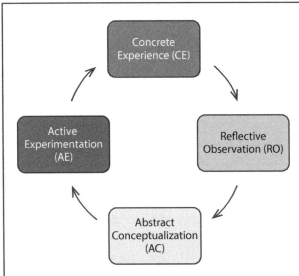

FIGURE 2. THE EXPERIENTIAL LEARNING CYCLE. (ADAPTED FROM KOLB, 1984)

d. Offer candy to the student volunteers who present their group's findings to the rest of the class.

5. Information Literacy Reflection *[Abstract Conceptualization]*
    a. Students reflect individually on the importance of evaluating information sources and predict what results they would retrieve in Google compared to the databases.
    b. Offer candy to the student volunteers who share their reflections.

6. Application *[Active Experimentation and Concrete Experience]*
    a. Assign each group a different resource to work with. Have students do a sample search using a keyword combination from the topic development activity to see what kind of

results are retrieved and what database features are available to assist in making their searches more accurate.
    ■ EBSCOhost, JSTOR, Google, and Google Scholar are resources to consider using because of their interdisciplinary nature.
    b. Have each group share their experience with their resource. A group spokesperson should answer the questions: What strategies did they use for searching? What features did they find? How credible are the results they retrieved? How accurate are the results they retrieved? Dialogue with each group to fill in any gaps present in order to make searching each resource more efficient.
    c. And, of course, offer candy to the student volunteers who present their group's findings to the rest of the class.

7. Self-Assessment *[Reflective Observation]*
    a. With a few minutes remaining at the end of the session, have students reflect on the session by answering the following questions on their notecards. Be sure to remind them that the notecards are anonymous and that the answers received will be used to enhance the course research guide.
    ■ From what you learned today, what will you use again?
    ■ What are you still troubled by?
    ■ What will your next steps be?
    b. Students should hand in their notecards as they leave the session

in exchange for one final round of candy for everyone.

ALLERGY WARNING
• In a 45–50-minute session, this becomes *very* fast paced. To save time, choose student volunteers instead of waiting for them to come forward and have fewer groups share on topic development and information literacy reflections.
• After the session, students still may not fully grasp the process of searching, gathering terms and other clues, re-searching, gathering more, and searching again. This cyclical search process is crucial to finding a workable search combination where a single set of results will not suffice. This point is stressed during several moments throughout the session.

CHEF'S NOTE
Take advantage of after-holiday candy sales to keep your supplies stocked.

ADDITIONAL RESOURCES
• Kolb, D.A. (1984). *Experiential learning: Experience as the source of learning and development*. Englewood Cliffs, NJ: Prentice-Hall.
• McLeod, S.A. (2013). Simply psychology: Kolb—learning styles. Retrieved from http://www.simplypsychology.org/learning-kolb.html.
• Manchester University first-year seminar Libguides. Retrieved from http://libguides.manchester.edu/fys.

Plagiarism Awareness for First-Year Students

Nancy Noe, Reference & Instruction Librarian, Auburn University, noenanc@auburn.edu

NUTRITION INFORMATION

Students in first-year programs often spend a class/unit on plagiarism. This recipe helps students develop their own definition of plagiarism, begin to recognize various examples of plagiarism, and internalize possible solutions for addressing the issue.

When asking librarians to cover plagiarism, many faculty mistakenly think that a one-shot session, mostly focused on formatting citations, is all students need to learn to avoid plagiarism. This session is an opportunity to begin a different conversation with faculty, one that begins to move the discussion past simple format into one that deals with the why, who, and how of the practice of scholarly writing. Be clear with the learning objective—this is a first step in *awareness*.

NUMBERS SERVED

4+ (Scalable)

COOKING TIME

50 to 75 minutes

ACRL FRAMEWORK ADDRESSED

Information Has Value

MAIN INGREDIENTS

- ☐ Teaching/presentation stations
- ☐ Whiteboards
- ☐ Bingo cards
- ☐ Prizes

MAIN COOKING TECHNIQUES

Think-pair-share, gaming, and problem-solving

PREPARATION

Create Bingo cards using an online Bingo card generator. Provide a copy for each student. Create a PowerPoint to guide the session. Article for summary.

COOKING METHOD

1. Introduction (5 minutes)
   a. Introduce self
   b. Briefly outline the day's session
2. Defining Plagiarism (10 minutes)
   a. Display the section of the Institution's Academic Policy code that relates to plagiarism.
   b. Group students in pairs, and using the Policy as their guide, ask them to write a definition of plagiarism in their own words, in a simple, single sentence.
   c. Ask each pair to share their sentences by writing on whiteboards or typing online for projection screen.
   d. Discuss commonalities.
3. Examples (10 minutes)
   a. Distribute Plagiarism Bingo cards to each students

b. Remind students of Bingo rules
   c. Have instructor "draw"
   d. First person to match wins a library prize
   e. Discuss examples: Were there any examples that surprised students or students questioned?
   f. Have students keeps their cards for future reference.
4. Citation Project (5 minutes)
   a. Explain Citation Project.
   b. Display graph of student use of sources in research papers.
   c. Discuss different ways students may use sources.
5. Solutions (10 minutes)
   a. In same pairs, ask students to brainstorm ways in which they can avoid plagiarism.
   b. Record suggestions on whiteboard or typing online for projection screen.
   c. Add important suggestions students might have missed.
   d. After class, e-mail students with a copy of the solutions and links to any other library information regarding plagiarism (videos, tutorials, LibGuide, etc.)
   e. Use solutions as an assessment of each class.

CHEF'S NOTES

For a 75-minute class, add to #4 above:

4.5. Summarizing Practice (10–15 minutes)

  a. Provide students with one-page article on plagiarism, focused on college students.

  b. Using carbonless paper, ask students to write a paragraph summarizing article.

  c. Review student work, share with instructor how well students did (assessment).

Scholars in Training:
Solving the Mystery

Jenny Yap, Librarian, Berkeley City College, jyap@peralta.edu; Sonia Robles, Adjunct Librarian, Berkeley City College srobles@ peralta.edu

NUTRITION INFORMATION

This recipe was created to introduce first-year English and ESL composition students to the differences between scholarly and popular sources. As an end of the semester assignment, all students taking English and ESL composition courses are required to write a research paper that incorporates the use of various types of sources, including scholarly sources. Students typically have never read or seen a scholarly journal.

This recipe gives students hands-on experience in looking at, reading, and analyzing scholarly journals. It also gets them to compare the differences between types of sources. This activity can be done during a one-shot, but we typically used it during the second session of a two-session library instruction workshop.

NUMBERS SERVED

25 students

COOKING TIME

40 minutes

DIETARY GUIDELINES

This activity addresses some of the foundational aspects of information literacy, starting with recognizing definable elements within an academic or popular resource. Students critically analyze how each resource may or may not support their writing assignment as well as vet each resource's authority and bias. The collaborative aspect of the analysis also brings in each group member's knowledge-set into play, allowing for natural conversation and a peer learning environment.

ACRL FRAMEWORKS ADDRESSED

- Authority is Constructed and Contextual
- Information Has Value
- Scholarship as Conversation

MAIN INGREDIENTS

- ☐ Manila envelopes with copies of the prompt, clues, and sources
- ☐ The room should have movable chairs to facilitate group collaboration
- ☐ Whiteboard / blackboard

MAIN COOKING TECHNIQUE

Small group work, hands-on activity, and class discussion

PREPARATION

Prepare 6 large manila envelopes with each containing two sources—a scholarly journal and either a magazine or newspaper—the prompt for the exercise, and a small envelope containing a clue with a detective magnifying glass drawn on it. Materials are all pre-packed prior to dining time.

COOKING METHOD

Step 1 Activity Introduction (<5 minutes)

The head detective needs assistance from the rookie gumshoes to help solve the mystery of the unknown resources. Break up students into 6 groups of 3–5 and set timer for 10 minutes.

Step 2 (10 minutes)

Allow students to review the contents in the manila envelope that contains a scholarly and popular publication and the exercise prompt in Figure 1.

Each prompt has a different set of questions, so you can have groups look at different aspects of the sources, such as the subscription information, the publisher, and the background of the writers. You can also ask questions that have them think about why the publication exists, the use of advertisements, the design, and the reading level.

Students sometimes need encouragement to actually look at the inner contents of the sources provided. It's also fun to encourage them to try to read a paragraph from the scholarly source.

FIGURE 1. EXERCISE PROMPT

Dear student detectives,
Your librarian is suffering from a concussion after several ency-clopedias fell on her head. She was given the job to organize these materials but has lost the ability to categorize and correctly identify these publications. As rookie gumshoes, she needs your help in solving and identifying the enclosed resources. She be-lieves she has found the best and brightest students on campus to help her with her mission. Do not let her down! Good luck.

Instructions:
As a group, you have 10 minutes to look at the mystery items in the envelope and compare the two different sources you were given. Answer the following questions. If you need clues to help you identify the resource, you can open up the clue envelope. At the end of 10 minutes you will present your findings to the rest of the class.

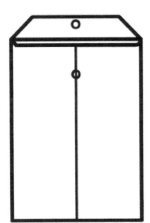

Questions:
1. What are the characteristics of the articles in the publications?
2. How much research do you think goes into each article?
3. Who reads these sources?

Clues

1. Look at the length of the articles in each source. Are there any charts, tables, graphs, or statistics? What type of subjects are these articles about?
2. Look at the citations (if there are any).
3. Think about what kind of knowledge you need to understand what the articles are talking about. Also look at whether or not the articles use a lot of specialized language or everyday language.

A clue is available within an envelope if stu-dents need additional help or guidance. This is optional as some students may choose to do the exercise without it. Some enjoy the challenge of not using the clue.

Step 3 (15 minutes)
The instructor draws a line down the middle of the board and labels one Scholarly and one Popular. Once time is up, ask each group (one by one) what noticeable differences appeared to them between their sources. (If you have extra time, students can also write down the differences on the board during Step 2.)

As the instructor records their responses on the board, the instructor asks questions prompting answers for any additional fea-tures students may have missed.

Step 4 (5 minutes)
Tie in the importance of each kind of source when doing research for an academic-level paper and where these sources can be found. Also use this time for any Q&A that may result from the exercise.

ALLERGY WARNINGS
Students may come away from this exercise thinking popular sources are not quality materials for their research. It is important to clarify that there are very good uses for popular sources, but that they, as the researchers, need to develop their critical thinking skills to determine when to use popular sources. We also tell them that it's always important to use a mix of sources.

CHEF'S NOTE

We've used this activity in one-shots and multi-session library instruction sessions for first-year students and international students. This activity is a hit in every class we've tried it in—developmental classes, college-level, and ESL classes. This activity elicits excitement about scholarly sources because of their personal and educational interests in certain disciplines. Self-identification of "scholar in training" also increases students' awareness of academic expectations.

Apple Slices:
A Card-Matching Party Game about the Library

Kelly Giles, Applied Sciences Librarian, James Madison University Libraries & Educational Technologies (JMU LET), gileskd@jmu.edu; Kristen Shuyler, Director, Outreach & Partnerships, JMU LET, shuyleks@jmu.edu; Andrew Evans, Public Services Hiring Coordinator, JMU LET, evansam@jmu.edu; Jonathan Reed, Outreach Coordinator, JMU LET, reedjj@jmu.edu

NUTRITION INFORMATION

Inspired by the popular party games *Apples to Apples* and *Cards Against Humanity*, this is a fun and flexible small-group activity developed for use in library orientation sessions.

NUMBERS SERVED

3–8 students per set of cards; with multiple decks can serve 50 or more

COOKING TIME

15–30 minutes per game session

DIETARY GUIDELINES

This activity serves as a casual introduction to library terminology, resources, and policies, and is intended to help students overcome library anxiety. The subjective judging of answers allows inexperienced library users to participate in—and even win—the game.

MAIN INGREDIENTS

☐ Question and answer card decks
☐ Handout of questions and answers
☐ Space for students to sit in small groups

MAIN COOKING TECHNIQUE

Game-based learning

PREPARATION

☐ Write a set of questions addressing the content that you want to cover during the session. These should be direct, closed-ended questions such as, "Where should you go to check out DVDs?" For a 30-minute game, write 27 questions. Prepare a handout with the questions and correct answers.

☐ Create a deck of question cards and a deck of answer cards for each group of players. These should have different colors or designs to make it easy to tell the two decks apart. See Additional Resources for card creation tools, or design your own featuring school colors, mascots, etc. Nine poker-size playing cards (2.5"x 3.5") will fit onto a sheet of 8.5"x 11" cardstock.

☐ Question cards should be double-sided, with the answers printed on the backs. Answer cards should feature a heading with a brief answer (e.g. "Media Resources") and a smaller explanation or definition (e.g. "Located in the basement of Carrier Library"). The answer deck should include a correct answer card for each question, plus additional answers. The total number of answers should be at least four times the number of questions. The extra answers can provide factual information about the library and other campus resources, but the game is more fun if you include humorous answers as well. You can duplicate answer cards to fill out the deck.

COOKING METHOD

1. Have students split into small groups and give each group a deck of question cards and a deck of answer cards. Briefly explain the rules of the game.
2. Each player draws five answer cards at the beginning of the game. Players take turns serving as judge. The judge draws a question card, keeping the answer on the back hidden, and reads it aloud. The other players each select an answer card from their hand and give it to the judge face down. The judge shuffles the answers and reads them aloud, then chooses the best one. This may sometimes be the most plausible answer, and other times the funniest. Whoever played the best answer is the winner of the round. The judge awards the ques-

tion card to that player, who then reads the correct answer on the back aloud. All players except the current judge draw an answer card. The role of judge passes to the right and a new round begins. When all question cards have been played or time runs out, the player who has been awarded the most question cards wins.

3. Answer any remaining questions students may have. Distribute the question and answer handout as a reminder of what they have learned.

ALLERGY WARNINGS

Students may become caught up in playing and forget to read the correct answer at the end of each round. The librarian should circulate during the game to keep an eye on players and answer questions. For a large group, it's helpful to have multiple librarians or staff members present.

CHEF'S NOTE

This activity can be used as a stand-alone introduction to the library or as an icebreaker in an instruction session. To shorten the game, remove question cards from the deck.

ADDITIONAL RESOURCES

- *Cards Against Humanity* website with blank card templates, http://www.cardsagainsthumanity.com/.
- Fruit to Fruit Card Generator for creating *Apples to Apples* style images, http://a2a.browndogcomputing.com/.
- The Game Crafter offers on-demand printing of custom card decks, https://www.thegamecrafter.com/.

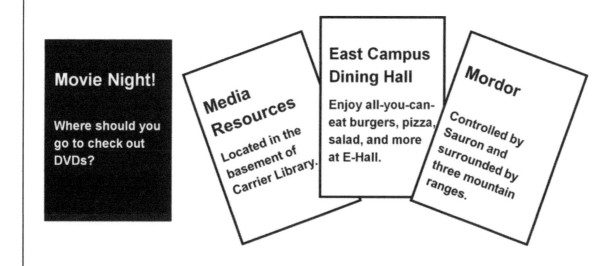

Writer:
Party of Two

Amanda B. Albert, Instructional Services Librarian, Saint Louis University, albertab@slu.edu

NUTRITION INFORMATION

Following this recipe over the course of two class sessions allows students to get a taste for basic library use and allows them to sample the skills that may be useful to them in future academic endeavors. They will begin with an appetizing discussion about information resources and end with the sweet taste of victory when they discover nutrition-packed information to use in their final projects.

This recipe was created to allow students to explore basic concepts within information literacy and provide them with the opportunity to explore the transferable skills they will need throughout their post-secondary education. Students are able to explore their own thoughts and feelings about information resources while also participating in what is often the first scholarly conversation with their peers.

NUMBERS SERVED

15–20 students

COOKING TIME

Approximately 50 minutes per session

DIETARY GUIDELINES

The larger purpose is to allow the students to interact with information resources in a way that they may not have in the past, while also allowing them to experience themselves as scholars and researchers on a topic.

ACRL FRAMEWORKS ADDRESSED

- Information Creation as Process
- Searching as Strategic Exploration
- Scholarship as Conversation

MAIN INGREDIENTS

- ☐ Flip chart and markers
- ☐ Whiteboard and markers
- ☐ Computers for student use
- ☐ Google Sheets

MAIN COOKING TECHNIQUES

Small group work, peer assistance, and mini lecture/demo

PREPARATION

- ☐ Gather ingredients
- ☐ Create the collaborative Google Sheet
- ☐ Share the Google Sheet with the students and instructor

COOKING METHOD

Instruction Session One:

1. Group discussion: Discuss Information Resources.
   a. Divide students into small groups (3–5).
   b. Assign each group a different information resource:
      - ○ Books
      - ○ Websites: Wikipedia, Google, and/or blogs
      - ○ Scholarly journal articles
      - ○ Newspaper/magazine articles
   c. Have them answer questions, i.e.:
      - ○ Who produces/authors?
      - ○ What is the purpose?
      - ○ Who gets paid?
      - ○ Where do you find this resource?
      - ○ Describe the contents
      - ○ How would you use this resource?
   d. Debrief, i.e.: What surprised you? Why do you think this way? How do you know? What does "scholarly" mean to you? Who gets paid?
2. Group discussion: Discuss how students find and use Information Resources.
   a. Engage the students about various resources.
      - ○ What do they think are appropriate uses for various resources? Why?
      - ○ How/where do they look for these resources?
3. Mini-lecture about using the library: Demonstrate search techniques.

a. Briefly demo how to find the resources we just talked about using the library.
b. Introduce using keywords to find information in a database.

Instruction Session Two:

1. Group brainstorm: Discuss the concepts of keyword creation and searching, delving deeper into this topic, and building upon the previous class session.
   a. Using a whiteboard, choose a student topic and break down that topic into searchable terms by asking for student input.
2. Small group work: Fill out the Google Sheet.
   a. Students pair up with a neighbor.
   b. Open up Google Sheet and fill in the first two boxes (Table 1).
   c. Students interview each other about their topics/thesis statement, and create 3–5 searchable terms.
   d. What is your topic?
   e. What do you already know?
   f. What do you still need to find out?
   g. Why do you care about this topic?
   h. Each student will find 1–2 relevant resources for their partner and input the MLA citation into the spreadsheet.
   i. Students evaluate the articles their partner found for them.
   j. Based off of these articles, students search for 1–2 more articles for themselves and complete the final two tasks.

3. Reflection: Written or verbal discussion.
   a. How did you feel about searching for information for your partner?
   b. Did it make you think about finding information in a new way?
   c. What else do you need to feel supported in your research?

ALLERGY WARNINGS

Students will give you answers they think you want to hear, so be sure to ask students probing questions to get at their deeper reasoning. Also, the Google Sheet activity varies in both time and attention, depending on how quickly students work and how much effort they put into evaluating the articles their partners found.

CHEF'S NOTE

- Providing specific examples for the resources activity makes this more concrete and applicable.
- The Google Sheet activity is adapted from the Project Cora Searching Strategically Sheet: http://www.projectcora.org/assignment/strategic-searching-spreadsheet.
- Adapt the questions on the spreadsheet, depending upon where the students are in the semester/progress of their assignment.
- Commenting on the students' work in the Google Sheet can happen in real time or after the instruction session as a follow up.

ADDITIONAL RESOURCES

Gardener, C. (2015). Strategic Searching Spreadsheet. *Community of Online Research Assignments*. Retrieved June 15, 2016 from http://www.projectcora.org/assignment/strategic-searching-spreadsheet.

TABLE 1. Searching As Strategic Exploration Spreadsheet							
Name	Thesis statement/ Topic statement	With your partner, list 3–5 possible search terms you might use to find sources.	Find a source that your partner may consider using in their research paper. Copy and paste the MLA citation below.	Describe how this article is relevant to your project.	What idea, source, or author do you want to find more about based on the source your partner just found?	Find two sources that you would consider using in your research paper. Copy and paste the MLA citations below.	Based on the results you found, list 2–3 other search terms you might use to find more sources.	Librarian Comments

Top Secret Recipes:
Internet Search Hacks Every Student Researcher Should Know

Amanda Foster, Instruction Librarian, Wake Forest University, fosterab@wfu.edu

NUTRITION INFORMATION

Students likely use the internet to find answers on a daily basis. This class asks students to explore the advanced search capabilities of Google and introduces them to free online research tools used by successful researchers. The ability to use advanced search techniques, whether on Google or in a library database, is a transferable skill and a great starting point for lifelong learning.

NUMBERS SERVED

Serves undergraduates in classes of 15–30

COOKING TIME

Cooking time is 50 to 75 minutes

ACRL FRAMEWORK ADDRESSED

Searching as Strategic Exploration

MAIN INGREDIENTS

- ☐ Internet access for all students
- ☐ Instructor computer with projector
- ☐ Wireless keyboard (optional)
- ☐ Worksheet with search prompts

MAIN COOKING TECHNIQUE

Active learning, small-group work, and small-group presentation

PREPARATION

Create instruction worksheets that contain a mixture of 10–12 advanced Google search techniques (see examples on *Power Searching with Google*) and useful free sites like The WayBack Machine, Google Books, Google Scholar, and Flickr Creative Commons. For each technique or site, provide detailed search prompts that include the exact search terms students should type into the search engine or research tool.

After each search prompt, ask at least one question that can only be answered by doing the search correctly. At the end of the worksheet, include a section with 5–6 "real world" search scenarios that ask students to apply the search techniques they've learned.

COOKING METHOD

1. Introduction. Open the session by discussing various search engines, focusing on Google. Note that by using advanced search techniques and online research tools, students can get "more" out of their online research.
2. Group work. Break students into 4–5 groups. Assign each group the task of learning 2–3 search techniques from the worksheet, usually 1–2 simple Google search techniques (e.g. the site: operator or limiting search results by date)

and one more complex research tool (e.g. The WayBack Machine). Let each group know that they will be expected to demonstrate their techniques and/or websites to the class, as this generally encourages them to be well-prepared.

3. Student presentations. Have each group give a short presentation on their 2–3 search techniques and online research tools. Encourage students to demonstrate actual searches, rather than just give a report. Since the worksheets include the search prompts for each group, invite the other students to fill out the answers on their worksheets as they follow along. When warranted, provide further information on a search tool or technique. For example, after having students demonstrate how to find images using the "labeled for re-use" search feature on Google Images, I have taken a few moments to discuss common ways students interact with copyrighted material and tips for how to do so legally and ethically.
4. Applied practice. After the groups have given demonstrations, ask each group to work through the "real world" search scenarios. This gives students the chance to apply their newly learned skills. For example, I've asked students to find examples of how local news

organizations in Baltimore were cover-
ing Freddie Gray in the days between
his arrest and death, which could be
answered using either the WayBack
machine or by limiting by date within
Google News.

ALLERGY WARNINGS
Search interfaces and results change over
time; run practice searches of all the search
prompts before the session begins.
Emphasize the importance of correct spac-
ing with advanced Google searching. For
example, when attempting to limit searches
using *site:.edu*, adding an extra space between site: and *.edu* can lead to inaccurate
search results.

CHEF'S NOTE
It can be fun to infuse relevant pop culture examples in addition to ways students
could use a particular technique or tool in
research. For example, MTV's *Catfish* makes
frequent use of Google's reverse image
search, but students could also use this tool
to locate the source of an image or find a
higher resolution version.

ADDITIONAL RESOURCES
- *Power Searching with Google*

Better Ingredients. Better Papers.

Jackie AlSaffar, Reference Librarian for External Services, Buena Vista University, alsaffarj@bvu.edu

NUTRITION INFORMATION

This recipe sells students on choosing nutritious sources, because just as "you are what you eat," student papers and projects are, in big part, the sources they use. Students have hopefully been exposed to a variety of sources throughout the years, yet they probably haven't had to think about how appropriate each might be as a source of information for an academic project. The idea is to evaluate sources beyond the rather simplistic "popular or scholarly?" conversation to a more graduated and nuanced appreciation of where each might exist on a continuum.

NUMBERS SERVED

Fewer than students 30 works best

COOKING TIME

15 minutes

DIETARY GUIDELINES

This activity asks students to assess the credibility of individual sources, ranking them on a continuum from least to most credible.

MAIN INGREDIENTS

- ☐ Handout: Multiple pre-made copies of the Credibility Continuum Scale (one for each group)
- ☐ Handout: Multiple sets of pre-made slips of paper, each with a source type/tool listed (one for each group)

MAIN COOKING TECHNIQUE

Small-group hands-on activity, discussion session

PREPARATION

- ☐ Librarian creates and prints off multiple copies of a "Credibility Continuum Scale" on 11 x 17 paper. The sheet is entitled: "How credible are your sources? Rate each by placing it on the continuum!" or similar wording. A double-arrowed line spans the page, in landscape layout. From left to right above the line are the words: Poor / Fair / Good / Very Good.
- ☐ Librarian types up and prints off multiple copies of a list of around 15 types of sources/tools, then cuts each into a thin slip of paper. Include a variety of sources (ingredients), from celebrity endorsements (junk food) to peer-reviewed articles (health foods). Some of the following "ingredients" might be considered for inclusion: Census Bureau; university-produced newspaper; editorial; Statistical Abstract of the United States; an organization (American Cancer Society, Livestrong, Sierra Club, United Way, Habitat for Humanity, etc.); peer-reviewed journal article; CNN transcript; think tanks (Cato Institute, Brookings Institution, Heritage Foundation, etc.); an ebook; a specialized online reference encyclopedia; someone's PowerPoint presentation found online; a YouTube video; a video from Films on Demand; a celebrity spokesperson; doctoral dissertation; a blog post; a documentary.

COOKING METHOD

The instruction session:

1. Students work in groups of two or three. Each group is given both handouts: the "Continuum Scale" and a batch of thin slips of paper, each listing a source.
2. They are given several minutes to position each slip of paper on the scale, where they think it belongs on the credibility scale from Poor to Very Good. Essentially, you're asking them to rank sources from least to most trustworthy.
3. Following this, a class discussion ensues. There is no one way to do this, but it works well to ask a single group where on the scale they put a particular source. Then ask other groups to indicate agreement or disagreement. There is no single right answer. If a group rates a source very differently than another, ask each why they rated it as they did.
4. Conclude by articulating the need to judge each source/tool on its merits, yet give them a sense that some sources/tools are, in general, better bets than others.

ALLERGY WARNINGS

Keep the activity moving along, taking care not to dwell on any one source/tool too long. However, if time permits, delve into sources they might be least familiar with, such as think tanks, editorials, and organizations. Choose a few sources to focus on, asking students when they would use each source and what its purpose is. Specifically, how would they use this source if they were writing an academic paper?

CHEF'S NOTE

Provide the reader with any additional information i.e. surprises, take-aways, personal experience with the activity, etc.

Librarians can tailor the ingredient list to include any sources or tools they deem appropriate or wish to acquaint students with.

- This is a great opportunity for librarians to illustrate that sources are not simply "good" or "bad," "black" or "white." A single source, such as an ebook, could appear anywhere along the continuum. First-year students may think of books primarily as novels they were required to read in high school, and have very little exposure to college-level, scholarly books.
- This activity can work well as a lead-in to a demo of a database, where students are asked to locate a particular source type (an editorial, a transcript, a university-produced newspaper, etc.).

- This activity could be modified to suit other continuums, such as a "Primary ↔ Secondary (↔ Tertiary) Continuum," whereby students are asked to rank sources according to what degree of "first-person voice" each has.

#Candy:
Creating Categories to Introduce Search Strategies

Elise Ferer, Librarian for Undergraduate Learning, Drexel University, etf25@drexel.edu; Kayla Birt Flegal, Access Services Librarian, DePauw University, kaylabirt@depauw.edu

NUTRITION INFORMATION

First-year students come into the academic library with varying levels of knowledge about how information is organized, whether that means books on the shelves, library websites, or databases. Knowing that there is an order to the information they are looking for can help them search more efficiently and strategically.

NUMBERS SERVED

Unlimited

COOKING TIME

50–75 minutes

DIETARY GUIDELINES

This recipe addresses the Searching as Strategic Exploration framework. If students are able to comprehend how information is organized, they can search for and discover relevant resources with greater success. Additionally, since information literacy instruction in the first year often happens in a first-year writing, composition, or seminar course, creating activities that are tied to the goals for college writing can help faculty see the benefits of information literacy instruction.

The Framework for Success in Postsecondary Writing places an importance on students "developing knowledge of writing conventions," which includes the global issues of organization of writing.[1] In developing creativity and flexibility in organization of ideas, students can use these skills to organize their writing as well as find information.

Students will:

- Comprehend how information is organized and that research is iterative in order to discover materials with more ease.
- Investigate the ways that organization shapes how we experience the world around us in order to apply it to writing for various academic and social audiences.
- Make connections between organizing for different audiences/types of information and writing for different audiences/genres and different writing conventions.

MAIN INGREDIENTS

- ☐ Candy or a suitable candy alternative (Legos, office supplies, etc.), with one "wildcard" item (we used raisins)
- ☐ Tabletops or space to organize and display candy
- ☐ Optional: device to take picture of results and/or post to a social media site

MAIN COOKING TECHNIQUE

Active learning, individual and group participation

PREPARATION

The preparation time for the librarian is about an hour, which could be longer, depending upon the elements (ingredients) the librarian chooses to add, such as homework. The librarian will need to gather materials that are being used in the lesson and prepare any extra information that will be used in class, such as handouts, extra questions, hashtags, etc.

COOKING METHOD

1. Hand out a variety of candy (or other items) to students and ask them to sort the items into categories as if they were creating their own candy store, and to consider how to organize their candy so their customers could find it easily.
2. After this, ask the students to form groups of 3–4, and as a group work to merge their "stores" and agree on one organization.
3. Assess how the groups decided to organize their "stores" via preferred method, either discussion, written reflection, or having students peer review others' organization methods. This can

spark great discussion among the class about methods and reasons for different organizations.

ALLERGY WARNINGS

This recipe relies heavily on student participation and students' abilities to work together in small groups.

CHEF'S NOTE

Additional steps may be added to the recipe including:

- The following step can be added to help students realize how organizational and folksonomic concepts extend into their online lives:
  - » Ask students to share their candy shops on social media using two hashtags, one created by the librarian and one created by each student or group of students.
  - » Ask students to add a sentence or two reflecting on how their candy store is organized.
- Peer review and feedback given without explanation by the group or student who organized the candy shop.
- Specific questions for discussion and reflection at the end of class, such as:
  - » Explain the process you used to organize your candy; also, how you merged your shop with that of your group. Was this easier or harder than you thought it would be?
  - » What surprised you about the way that other people organized their candy shops?

NOTES

1. Council of Writing Program Administrators, the National Council of Teachers of English, and the National Writing Project, *Framework for Success in Postsecondary Writing* (2011), accessed 27 April 2016, http://wpacouncil.org/files/framework-for-success-postsecondary-writing.pdf.

Grilling Sources for Information:
Determining which Ingredients Are Best

Heather Snapp, First Year Experience and Outreach Librarian, Florida Gulf Coast University, hsnapp@fgcu.edu

NUTRITION INFORMATION

First-year students are often not sure where to start in doing research or how different types of sources can serve different information needs. This activity allows them to physically see and explore a variety of sources and discuss situations when each might be used. Grilling sources before using them helps add to their nutritional value when they are used in essays or research projects.

NUMBERS SERVED

A group of 24 is ideal; if more need to be served, multiple grilling stations of the same source can be added as necessary.

COOKING TIME

50–60 minutes

DIETARY GUIDELINES

All students should have healthy doses of the ACRL frames to give them a foundation for information literacy.

ACRL FRAMEWORKS ADDRESSED

- Authority is Constructed and Contextual
- Information Creation as a Process
- Information Has Value

MAIN INGREDIENTS

- ☐ Self-stick flip chart paper (25" x 30")
- ☐ Small sticky notes (3" x 3")
- ☐ Markers (one color for each group)
- ☐ A variety of sources: Encyclopedia, book, newspaper, magazine, journal, webpage printout
- ☐ A handout with instructions for the carousel activity
- ☐ A space with ample room for groups to move around to multiple stations

MAIN COOKING TECHNIQUE

Small group carousel, whole class discussion

PREPARATION

- ☐ Place grilling stations around the room, each with the following: a different source, flip-chart paper on the wall or table, a different colored marker.
- ☐ Create approximately 30 information needs on small sticky notes and put in stacks for each group. (Examples: definition of ammonium chloride; research study on how online learning affects GPA; history and in-depth discussion of issues in higher education; opinion article on a current controversy, etc.)
- ☐ Create handout with questions that students will need to answer. Alterna-

tively, these could be projected for all to see. (See Cooking Method, Part I #3.)

COOKING METHOD
Part I

1. Begin with a brief whole-class discussion on sources to gauge previous knowledge. Ask the question: What sources are you familiar with, and which would you turn to when writing an academic research paper?
2. Divide the class into groups of about 3–5 students each. The number of groups can vary and will correspond with the number of sources to which you would like to introduce them.
3. Ask students to explore the source at their station and write on the flip chart paper the following information about their source in 5 minutes:
   a. What are the source's physical features?
   b. What, in general, are its contents?
   c. Why would someone want to read it?
   d. Who writes it?
   e. Who reads it?
   f. Where can you obtain it?
   g. What are some example titles?

4. Carousel time! Taking their colored marker with them, each group will rotate clockwise and have 2 minutes to review and add to each flip chart, such as:
   a. Emphasizing points the previous groups made (underlining, smiley faces, exclamation points, etc.—drawing pictures is encouraged!)
   b. Adding new or important ideas
   c. Using question marks if they think a previous idea might be incorrect or needs further discussion
5. When groups get back to their initial chart, a whole-class discussion on each source is led by each of the groups to summarize key points for each source and address any disagreements.

Part II

1. Give each group a stack of small sticky notes that you wrote the information needs on; you can also leave a few blank for them to write their own.
2. As a group, students decide in which source they would find each piece of information and put the sticky note on the corresponding flip chart.
3. Groups stand by their original charts for a whole-class debriefing. This last discussion is particularly rich. Some of the information needs can, of course, be found in different sources. Good conversations usually ensue about which sources to turn to for different information or points of view.

4. To test for individual understanding, a paper or online assessment can be given asking students to match up characteristics and information needs with sources.

ALLERGY WARNINGS

- Give verbal instructions to students *before* they break up into their stations. Once they begin, it can be difficult to get their attention.
- As the facilitator, you might need to point out characteristics that students miss, especially when it comes to journals. Pointing out references, author credentials, etc. is essential for this activity.

CHEF'S NOTE

Short on time? Here are some variations. Part I of this activity can be done on its own. Alternatively, characteristics of the sources can be provided for brief review before jumping into Part II. I have also separated these parts into two different class sessions when given the opportunity to attend the class twice.

Really short on time? Instead of having students move around the room, they can form groups at a table with all the sources in front of them and a handout in which they fill in the characteristics and information needs.

Google Bytes:
Chowing Down on the One-Shot Information Literacy Session for First-Year Students

Carly Lamphere, Librarian, Instruction and Reference Services, The Fashion Institute of Design and Merchandising, clamphere@fidm.edu

NUTRITION INFORMATION

First-year students tempted to begin and end their research for projects using Google usually do so out of familiarity with the search engine. However, projects prepared solely from Google resources often yield bittersweet final grades. Instead of stomaching the bland results yielded from unseasoned Google usage, this recipe teaches students fast and easy search strategies to spice up search results. These quick dishes introduce basic search concepts and tools to students while they utilize Google, Google Images, Google Scholar, and Google News. With minimal preparation, these 10-minute recipes will not only produce higher quality sources from Google, they also teach students strategies to nosh on later when browsing the library's subscription research databases.

NUMBERS SERVED

26–28 students at a time

COOKING TIME

10–30 minutes, depending on how many recipe versions are requested

MAIN INGREDIENTS

- ☐ One to two librarians
- ☐ One video projector/screen
- ☐ One computer with internet access
- ☐ Print copies of the recipe(s) for students to take home

MAIN COOKING TECHNIQUE

Lecture and demonstration and discussion

PREPARATION

- ☐ Set up projector and internet with Google, Google Image, Google Scholar, or Google News as the homepage, depending on the audience's recipe preferences.
- ☐ Distribute recipe(s) for students to follow along while the librarian gives a cooking demonstration.

COOKING METHOD

This recipe varies in flavors and cook time, depending on what the students and instructor are interested in tasting. For each variation, begin with introductions from the librarian(s) and ask students if they use Google as a source for research. They may be reluctant to admit how often they use Google for their research. However, reassure them that Google is a wonderful ingredient for cooking a five-star dish, but it often falls short of creating a satisfying meal. Segue into other ingredients (i.e., Google search options) based on dietary preferences:

Option 1: "Become a Power Searcher"

- Begin with throwing Boolean search operators in word and symbol form (And, Or, Not / ( ), " ", -) in a pan and bring to boil.
- Add a search topic and stir in the operators to narrow/adjust the number of search results. For example:
  - » gun violence
  - » gun violence "statistics"
  - » gun violence "statistics"—NRA
- Simmer on low until ready to serve with a side explanation of how these search operators work in the library research databases as well.

Option 2: "Reverse Image Search and Google Images"

- Begin a reverse image search:
  - » Pull an image from a news article found on Google.
  - » Save the image to the desktop.
  - » Upload the image into Google Images by clicking on the camera displayed in the search bar.
- Taste the results.
- Adjust the reverse image search results using the available filtering options. For example:
  - » Enter "Calvin Klein" as a search topic into the Google Image search bar.

» Remove from stove and strain search results using one or more of the available filtering options, such as "Color," "Size," and "Usage rights").

- Sprinkle in a discussion of alternative fair-use image sites like Wikimedia Commons into the skillet, along with reverse image search and basic image search filters, and simmer until ready to serve.

Option 3: "Google Scholar and News"

- In Google Scholar, begin with a broad topic (like "child labor") to sauté.
- Uncheck the "include patents" box.
- Taste the search results.
- Garnish with explanations of how to locate full-text articles as well as where to locate the citation tool.
- This recipe can also be used in Google News:
  - » Adjust the search results by selecting "More" and using the down arrow to filter results (e.g., "Recent" and "Relevance").
- Cover Google Scholar and Google News search results until ready to serve.

ALLERGY WARNINGS

Live demonstrations can yield unexpected results. To insure successful recipe demonstrations, practice different topics/terms/ingredients to gain confidence with each recipe in case of undesired flavors or reactions.

CHEF'S NOTE

Student experience with these recipes will vary. Conduct a temperature check after introducing each cooking method to gauge student understanding. If most students are familiar with the recipe, focus on more complex flavors. To keep students engaged, choose search topics/terms/ingredients according to student interest or course assignment.

A Reserved Table for First-Generation Students

Neal Baker, Library Director, Earlham College, bakerne@earlham.edu; Jane Marie Pinzino, Academic Outreach Librarian, Earlham College, pinzija@earlham.edu

NUTRITION INFORMATION

More than a recipe, this is a menu prepared for first-generation students in their initial semester. It enables them to identify library resources and services that will help them analyze trending issues and current events. At the same time, it teaches academic research "etiquette" while finding, using, and sharing information. In a weekly, small table setting, first-generation students form a peer cohort and get to know a librarian while reflecting on the technology affordances of complimentary mobile devices, together with peer feedback and short writing assignments. The goals are to help retain first-generation students in general, and to introduce library research in particular.

NUMBERS SERVED

5–10 students per section; a total of 20–30 students every initial semester

COOKING TIME

90 minutes per week, per section, for 7 weeks; can be adjusted as needed

DIETARY GUIDELINES

The initiative aligns the library with the college's commitment to student diversity, while demonstrating the value of the library to student retention.

ACRL FRAMEWORKS ADDRESSED

- Research as Inquiry
- Searching as Strategic Exploration
- Information Has Value

MAIN INGREDIENTS

- ☐ Librarian dedication and time
- ☐ Complimentary mobile devices for all students (optional)
- ☐ Classroom reservations

MAIN COOKING TECHNIQUE

Small group discussions, hands-on mobile device work, and reflection

PREPARATION

Any menu catered to a specific group (e.g. first-generation students) must be marketed and coordinated. Key tasks include recruiting students (in our case, with help from the Registrar's Office and athletic coaches), ordering mobile devices, scheduling sections, and learning about the invitees.

COOKING METHOD

(Examples, not in any particular sequence)

Session A

- Students research a current event/issue relevant to themselves (e.g. alcohol use in college, student debt).
- Locate information from popular news sources, plus peer-reviewed articles from library databases.
- Present information to class using mobile device.
- Presenters identify differences between source types.
- Peer feedback.
- Discussion about each topic and its implications for college life.

Session B

- Students each find a mobile app to support their college success.
- Students demonstrate their selected apps to class.
- Discussion of apps.

Session C

- Students write an in-class paragraph about "being first" (e.g. first in line, first in competitions, first in birth order, first in family to attend college).
- Share paragraphs (with partner, with entire class).
- Focus discussion on the distinctive experiences of being first in family to attend college.
- Together address query: What unique perspectives and contributions come with being the first in family to college? (e.g. at school, at home).

Final session
- Celebratory meal for all sections together with campus partners and guests (e.g. Senior Associate Director of Athletics, Associate Dean of Student Life, and Director of Diversity and Inclusion).

ALLERGY WARNINGS
Our menu is expensive: roughly $500 per student (mobile device, accessories, final meal). Any institution could modify the menu without devices or the meal. The key ingredients are dedicated librarians to work with small groups.

CHEF'S NOTE
- Forget the adage about too many cooks spoiling things; this menu has always relied on campus partners. Ours include the Registrar's Office (scheduling, advocacy), the Academic Dean and Vice President of Academic Affairs (funding, advocacy), the campus McNair Scholars Program (consulting on best practices, destination for qualified students), and academic advisers and athletic coaches (recruitment).
- Our menu began as library-centric, but after three years is purposely integrating more partners (e.g. the Director of the McNair Scholars Program, the Director of the Writing Center, and a Senior Associate Vice President for Academic Affairs will be section instructors working on the information literacy framework from their own vantages).

- Our initiative attracted the generosity of an alumna donor, who will fund $40,000 per year for the next three years to add an all-expenses-paid, 2–3 week off-campus program for select, first-generation students led by a librarian-faculty pair at the end of a cohort's freshman year.
- To bridge the initial semester section and the summer off-campus program, select, first-generation students will undertake a for-credit research tutorial/project in spring semester related to the off-campus program location. The tutorial/project will be under the instruction of a librarian.

ADDITIONAL RESOURCES
For more details about the program, see: http://library.earlham.edu/LIFT.

Database Dash

Amy Gratz, Learning and Teaching Services Librarian, Horace W. Sturgis Library, Kennesaw State University, agratz1@kennesaw.edu

NUTRITION INFORMATION

This activity introduces students to the variety of resources and useful features available in databases, and was developed as an alternative to the standard database demonstration. A cross between Bingo and a scavenger hunt, small groups of students compete to complete as many tasks as possible in five minutes. The competitive nature of the activity is highly engaging!

NUMBERS SERVED

8–20 students

COOKING TIME

10–15 minutes

DIETARY GUIDELINES

This recipe was designed to be used as a single component of an instruction session following an introduction to other necessary knowledge practices.

ACRL FRAMEWORK ADDRESSED

Searching as Strategic Exploration, allowing students to begin developing the following knowledge practices:

- Design and refine needs and search strategies as necessary, based on search results.
- Understand how information systems are organized in order to access relevant information.

- Use different types of searching language appropriately.
- Manage searching processes and results efficiently.

MAIN INGREDIENTS

- ☐ Computer with projector
- ☐ 4 to 5 computers (one per group)
- ☐ Sticky notes in different colors (one pad per group)
- ☐ Timer
- ☐ Space for students to easily access the presentation screen
- ☐ Paper for keeping score
- ☐ Prizes

MAIN COOKING TECHNIQUE

Small group activity, some class discussion

PREPARATION

- ☐ Create a presentation slide with the following rules:
  - » Work in [database] on the topic "[instructor's choice here]"
  - » Only one computer per group
  - » After completing each task, send a group member up to place a sticky note on the appropriate square(s)
  - » Bingos are counted double!
- ☐ Develop a list of 24 discreet tasks, such as "locate a magazine article," that students can complete in the chosen database. In a second presentation

slide, arrange these in a 5×5 Bingo board, placing a "free space" in the center.
- ☐ Print one handout per group with a copy of the Bingo board and the rules of the game.
- ☐ Prepare a score-pad for use during the session.
- ☐ Immediately before the session, prepare the timer for 5 minutes.

COOKING METHOD

1. Set-up: With your rules slide displayed, go over the activity and divide students into groups of about three, handing out the sticky notes. Students should take on specific roles: the "researcher" operates the computer, the "runner" places sticky notes on the presentation board, and the "coordinator" keeps track of progress using the worksheet. Any additional students should be "spotters," helping the researcher complete the different tasks. Researchers should access the database search page now.
2. Main activity: Once all groups are ready, distribute handouts, switch to the Bingo board slide, and start the timer. Supervise each group to minimize opportunities for cheating—and cheer them on!
3. Scoring/awards: Once time has run out, score each group as follows: One point per task and five point bonuses per

Bingo completed. The group with the most points wins! Hand out prizes.

4. Review: Discuss with the students what they learned, which tasks were most difficult, and any questions they have. Demonstrate any tasks that were either not completed or were particularly confusing.

ALLERGY WARNINGS

- Because this activity is timed, it promotes quantity over quality. It works well for introducing students to a wide variety of resources/tools, but is not appropriate for requiring students to locate high-quality sources.
- Students will often assume they are finished as soon as they get Bingo. Remind them that the goal is to complete as many tasks as they can, not just get five in a row.
- Student teams that fall behind can lose motivation to continue playing. You can counter this by including a cooperative "black-out" component, where the entire class works together to complete every task on the board. Include a secondary prize to be awarded if each task is completed by at least one team, and consider providing one minute of bonus time to achieve this goal.

CHEF'S NOTE

- This activity is very engaging and a lot of fun! I have had several professors tell me that it involved students who were typically not very engaged in the class.

- After completing the activity, I typically do a *very brief* demonstration in a different database, to show that similar tools are available in any library database.
- Identifying 24 tasks to complete in a single database can be difficult. If necessary, create a smaller board, such as 4×4. You will need to adjust the amount of competition time to maintain the challenge.
- I enjoy highlighting some unexpected features of databases, such as the "find a source published in 2016" task in the example, which was used in the fall of 2015. This gave me an opportunity to discuss with the students how the publishing process works.
- Highlight particularly important skills and make these tasks worth 2 points instead of 1 to encourage completion. (In the example, the shaded squares were considered the most important.)
- Inexpensive prizes, such as notebooks and pens, work well for this activity. I often keep the prizes a secret until awarding them; students are competitive even when the reward is a surprise!

ADDITIONAL RESOURCES

- This activity was also presented at the Atlanta Area Bibliographic Instruction Group Conference 2016. The presentation is available at www.slideshare.net/ agratz/innovative-database-instruction- bingo.

RESEARCH BINGO: Search Discovery

LIMIT THE SUBJECT TO "ETHICS" OR "BIOETHICS"	USING DISCOVERY, FORMAT AN MLA STYLE CITATION FOR AN ARTICLE	FIND A "RESEARCH STARTER"	FIND A DVD	LIMIT YOUR SEARCH BY LANGUAGE (ENGLISH ONLY PLEASE!)
FIGURE OUT HOW TO REQUEST A BOOK FROM THE SWILLEY (ATLANTA) LIBRARY	FIND A BOOK REVIEW	FIND A BOOK IN THE MERCER UNIVERSITY LIBRARIES	LIMIT YOUR SEARCH TO THE LIBRARY CATALOG	GET LESS THAN 1 THOUSAND SEARCH RESULTS
FIND AN EBOOK	FIND A PDF FOR A SCHOLARLY ARTICLE	**FREE SPACE**	FIND RESOURCES ABOUT A FOREIGN COUNTRY	FIND AN IMAGE OR PIECE OF ARTWORK
FIND A CURRENT NEWS ARTICLE	GET MORE THAN 2 MILLION SEARCH RESULTS	FIND A MAGAZINE ARTICLE	FIND SOMETHING PUBLISHED IN 2016	EMAIL AN ARTICLE WITH AN MLA CITATION
CHECK YOUR SEARCH HISTORY	LIMIT YOUR SEARCH TO FULL TEXT ONLY	FIND AN ARTICLE USING THE ORANGE "FIND FULL TEXT" BUTTON	LIMIT THE PUBLICATION DATE TO THE LAST 5 YEARS	FIND AN ARTICLE WITH HTML FULL-TEXT

Indulging in Infographics:
Research Presentations for First-Year Students

Myra Waddell, Instruction and Research Support Librarian, University of Hawai'i at Mānoa, waddellm@hawaii.edu

NUTRITION INFORMATION

The goal of this recipe is to teach first-year students how to create meaningful research projects using infographics. First-year students who are required to complete research projects with a visual component will benefit from *Indulging in Infographics*.

At the University of Hawai'i at Mānoa, information literacy instruction on infographics is embedded into Oceanography and Global Environmental Science (OCN 100). Library instruction for OCN 100 is served in three courses, evenly staggered over a semester. By the end of the third course, students are satiated from digesting nutritious infographic know-how and powered-up to create deliciously digital research presentations.

NUMBERS SERVED

20–30 students per class

COOKING TIME

Three cooking sessions, each lasting 50–60 minutes

DIETARY GUIDELINES

The larger purpose of this recipe is to give first-year students experience with using technology tools to communicate their research findings in a non-traditional, visual, and digital format. Since digital forms of communication are used more frequently in academics and in the professional world, students will benefit from understanding how to create infographics and use them to convey ideas. Likewise, as digital communication changes overtime, so will the ways in which information is organized and depicted. Teaching students to use new technology tools in tandem with teaching ways to clearly communicate textual and visual information is essential to keeping current with evolving communication methods.

Utilizing infographics to convey specific messages, tell a story, or relay facts helps teach students that research, revising, and displaying information is a creative process, where the information output or product can take on a variety of formats.

ACRL FRAMEWORK ADDRESSED

* Information Creation as a Process

MAIN INGREDIENTS

☐ Library subject guide containing information on infographics
☐ Student handouts
☐ A variety of sample infographics to use during class discussion

☐ Instruction classroom or computer lab with enough desktop computers or laptops for each student
☐ Instructor station with computer and projector
☐ Internet access
☐ Access to Piktochart.com

MAIN COOKING TECHNIQUE

Librarian-chefs utilize a combination of cooking techniques to ensure a well-rounded, flavorful experience.

* Active learning: The majority of this cooking experience includes hands-on learning, where students examine infographic examples, explore how to manipulate an infographic creation tool, search for information to use in their own infographic, and populate their infographic with text and imagery.
* Group discussion: Librarian facilitates two group discussions: one discussion on infographic design and another discussion during a peer review process.
* Student reflection: Students reflect on their own infographic design, as well as their peers' work.
* Technology demonstration: Librarian briefly demonstrates an infographic creation tool.

PREPARATION

To make this cooking experience run as smoothly as possible, a LibGuide and student handout can be prepared in advance.

LibGuide: Craft the LibGuide to be as concise or as elaborate as needed to enhance the tastes of this session. The LibGuide should include in the least:
- ☐ Links to Piktochart.com and other infographic tools
- ☐ A variety of infographic examples
- ☐ Links to library resources suited to the topic needs of the class
- ☐ Resources to digital information use and ethics

Student handout: Use as a compliment to the LibGuide. Student handout can include:
- ☐ Links to the library session LibGuide and infographic tools
- ☐ Space for students to jot down notes during the session activities
- ☐ A description of infographic project goals and outcomes
- ☐ Homework reminders and expectations

COOKING METHOD

First course appetizers: Munching on digital presentation basics

1. Infographic bites. At the beginning of the first course, the librarian defines *infographic* and shows a variety of examples. Next, working in groups, students identify the main topic or theme of each example and list their defining characteristics. Students also critically examine each infographic's organizational structure. After discussing, groups share their findings with the class. Then, as a class, conclusions on how successful each infographic conveys information are made.

2. Topic sampler platter. During the second portion of the appetizer course, students explore potential topics to use for creating an infographic. Topics should align with themes covered in class (in this case, ocean and environmental science topics). Working individually, but with freedom to discuss ideas with classmates, students search library databases, online media, popular online journals, and digital image resources to gather ideas. At this time, the librarian assists with the search process, addresses student needs, and instructs on how to make wise resource choices.

3. Flavor infused homework. In preparation for the second course, students find sources (including images) related to their topic that they will incorporate into their own infographic.

Second course salad bar: Build-your-own infographic

1. A handful of greens. At the beginning of course two, the librarian briefly demonstrates Piktochart, a free online infographic tool. The demonstration works best when only key features are pointed out.

2. Sprinkle on the toppings. The goal during the second portion of course two is for students to create an infographic that expresses their personal interest in their chosen topic and communicates related scientific information. Student infographics will show an organized flow of information and will display:
   - » Title of research topic or theme
   - » Why the topic is important in global environmental science
   - » Examples of existing research on the topic

3. Working individually, students experiment with Piktochart and begin to design their infographic. Take note that this process may be confusing or challenging to students who are inexperienced with technology or who are not accustomed to abstract, visual thinking. It may be helpful for students to roughly sketch out their ideas on scratch paper and then transfer these ideas to the infographic. While students work, the librarian circulates the room, helps students manipulate Piktochart, and assists with incorporating sources and organizing information.

4. Flavor infused homework. Students add content to their infographic and prepare to present their work during the third course.

Third course entrée: Infographic evaluation and ethics

1. Feasting on feedback. The entrée course focuses on the completed infographics and evaluation. In small groups, students share their infographics and receive feed-

back from group members. The librarian facilitates the feedback process by encouraging students to make positive objective statements of value. Optional: the librarian can share how to give effective feedback by distributing examples of positive feedback statements to the class before they form groups.

2. Drizzle on the ethics. After small group sharing, the class comes together to discuss information ethics. The librarian builds off earlier discussions and prompts the class to further examine the ethics related to using information in a digital context. This discussion may include a mixture of the following:
   » Finding and using copyright-free images
   » Accurate ways to cite text and images in infographics
   » Intellectual freedom and ownership of digital objects
   » Social and personal implications of using infographic tools
   » Social and personal implications of sharing information digitally

3. During the ethics discussion, students are encouraged to reflect on how they might change their infographic to better mirror their values concerning information creation, organization, dissemination, and use.

ALLERGY WARNINGS

- Experience with this recipe has shown students need a lot of time to explore the infographic tool and get used to its features. Plan for extra time to allow students to explore and work out the kinks that come with learning a new technology tool.

- The exercises in this recipe require students to think in a visual way that is more abstract than what they may be used to. It is helpful to explain to students that learning new technology and thinking in abstract ways are processes that may require extra time.

CHEF'S NOTE

This three-course recipe can be consolidated to fit the one-shot instruction model. For this scenario, it can be helpful to collaborate with the course instructor on incorporating various elements of the library session into class lectures prior to meeting for the workshop. For example, the librarian and instructor can prep students on the nature of infographics (see *Infographic bites* from the first course). This preliminary work could be done in the class lecture or embedded in an online course management system (CMS), where the librarian supplies materials and discussion prompts for the lecture or the CMS.

Another possibility has the course instructor work with students prior to the library session to choose suitable research topics. The librarian can request the instructor email a list of topics to her in advance. Having the topics ahead of time frees up valuable workshop time and allows space for the librarian to prepare potential resources suited to student research topics.

ADDITIONAL RESOURCES
Infographic tools:
- Piktochart https://piktochart.com/
- Venngage https://venngage.com/
- Infogram https://infogr.am/
- Easelly http://www.easel.ly/

Sample infographics to use for class discussion and critique:
- Daily Infographic http://www.dailyinfographic.com/
- Good https://www.good.is/infographics

Other resources
- The Slow Journalism Company http://www.slow-journalism.com/filter/infographics
- *ACRL Framework for Information Literacy for Higher Education,* http://www.ala.org/acrl/standards/ilframework

From Prep to Delivery:
Peer Instruction for First-Year Business Students

Teresa Williams, Business Librarian, Butler University Libraries, twilliam@butler.edu

NUTRITION INFORMATION

This recipe highlights the value of peer instruction for students in a First-Year Business Experience (FBE) course. Follow these steps to prepare upper-level business majors to serve as Peer Instructors who will co-teach with the Librarian to share a "tried and true" recipe for research success in an important first-year course.

NUMBERS SERVED

Serves up to 25 first-year business students

COOKING TIME

Allow up to 2 hours for prep and 1 hour for classroom delivery

DIETARY GUIDELINES

This recipe has a positive impact on student learning in two ways. First, it provides an opportunity for upper-level business majors to share their knowledge and gain teaching experience through targeted peer instruction. It also introduces first-year students to an investigative method for finding and evaluating business information, with an emphasis on documenting the research path for further exploration and citation of sources.

ACRL FRAMEWORK ADDRESSED

Searching as Strategic Exploration

MAIN INGREDIENTS

- ☐ Upper-level business major who successfully completed the FBE course
- ☐ Classroom or lab
- ☐ Instructor's station with document camera
- ☐ Computer access for students
- ☐ Selected tutorials on business information resources
- ☐ Course LibGuide
- ☐ Reliable resources for business information
- ☐ Search Log with columns for "Information Needed," "Resource Consulted," "Search Terms Used," and "What You Found."

MAIN COOKING TECHNIQUE

Librarian and Peer Instructor combine discussion/demo with hands-on research and team consultations

PREPARATION

Recruit an upper-level business major who completed the FBE course. Note: Prep time is shorter with students who work in the Library's Information Commons program, but the Librarian may substitute other qualified business majors. In collaboration with FBE faculty, post tutorials on business information resources to the course management system for FBE students to review prior to the in-class instruction session. The Peer Instructor will review the same tutorials and practice completing a Search Log to record the results of sample searches for business information.

COOKING METHOD

1. Introductions and testimonial: 5 minutes

   a. The Librarian introduces the Peer Instructor who will identify his/her major, year in the degree program, and the professor who taught his/her FBE course.

   b. The Peer Instructor then talks about his/her personal experience in the course, including the value of the instruction session, and reveals how his/her first-year team fared in the course business plan competition. The Peer Instructor also highlights how the session contributes to better research outcomes in upper-level business courses.

2. Show-and-tell: 20 minutes

   a. The Peer Instructor distributes blank Search Logs to the students.

b. The Librarian discusses course project and research strategies as the Peer Instructor documents the process on a Search Log. Students may add notes to their own Search Logs to help them recall the process.

c. After two or three resources are reviewed, the Peer Instructor uses the document camera to show students the research path as tracked on the Search Log. He/she points out how one source may lead to discovery of another or why some entries may be crossed off the Search Log as the research progresses.

d. The steps are repeated until a variety of reliable business information sources are introduced, discussed, and documented.

3. Hands-on research and team consultation: 35 minutes

a. Following show-and-tell, students work in teams to identify information needs for their business plan. Team members use the course LibGuide to explore resources demonstrated in the session and record their efforts on their Search Logs.

b. As students conduct research, the Librarian and Peer Instructor meet briefly with each team to answer questions and provide encouragement.

4. Follow-up: Until done (time varies)

a. Scan the sample Search Log completed by the Peer Instructor during the session and save it to the course LibGuide for later reference.

b. The Peer Instructor may volunteer to assist the Librarian with open lab sessions held for the FBE students the week before assignment is due.

ALLERGY WARNINGS

Make sure the Peer Instructor not only knows the material but is also comfortable speaking in front of a class. Carefully monitor time devoted to show-and-tell to allow for quality team consultations. (Assigning tutorials prior to the session helps with time constraints). Remind students that research is an exploratory process, and their completed Search Logs will vary in terms of paths taken and sources recorded.

CHEF'S NOTE

The "testimonial" from the Peer Instructor is an important element of this recipe. The first-year students sit up and pay attention when they realize they are getting advice from a fellow student who can relate to their situation and has achieved success in the same course. The peer instruction has also been well-received by the FBE faculty.

The Business Librarian and Information Commons Librarian at Butler University collaborated to integrate the Peer Instructor component into the FBE course. Many of the Information Commons students involved say the opportunity helped them learn more about business information re-

sources and gave them a greater appreciation of the effort involved in preparing and providing information literacy instruction.

ADDITIONAL RESOURCES

- "Trade Sources"—One of the tutorials reviewed by first-year business students prior to in-class instruction session. http://www.guideside.palni.org/guide_on_the_side/tutorial/tradepubs.
- Blank Search Log.
- Search Log completed by the Peer Instructor during instruction session
- Three photos of Peer Instructor demonstrating a Search Log used to track the research process.

Chefs Academy:
Creating a Scenario-based Activity for First-Year Engineering Students
Chris Langer, Public Services Librarian, California State University–Fresno, clanger@csufresno.edu

NUTRITION INFORMATION
Cooking for first-year engineering students is notoriously difficult. Traditional research papers requiring library resources are a rare dish in a curriculum that is heavy on hands-on projects and labs. By using a collaborative, scenario-based activity in your instruction session, you can enliven your engineering one-shot by utilizing a format that engineering students are comfortable with as the power of peer-learning turns them into the chefs!

NUMBERS SERVED
Unlimited

COOKING TIME
Flexible, as the recipe can be easily adapted for 50–75 min sessions

DIETARY GUIDELINES
This recipe is designed to serve information literacy skills to students in introductory courses with no research assignment. With a little creativity, most learning objectives can be adapted to this recipe.

MAIN INGREDIENTS
☐ One computer lab
☐ One librarian
☐ Class of first-year engineering students
☐ Worksheet handouts

☐ LibGuide (optional)

MAIN COOKING TECHNIQUE
Small group work, peer-learning, and short presentations

PREPARATION
Preparation is key for this recipe. For the dish to turn out right, you need to develop a set of scenarios that turn your learning objectives into realistic problems that your first-year engineering students will need to solve. Do you want your students to learn how to use Engineering Village? You could write up a scenario where the student is a research assistant for a professor who wants them to find the full text of several articles they wrote years back. Want to teach your students about interlibrary loan? Make them find a transportation-planning book that *just so happens* to be unavailable at the library. Want your students to learn about the technology that is available for checkout? Perhaps their student organization needs to find a data projector for a big presentation. Be creative!

The handout you create should lay out the scenarios and include space for answers, but also include your contact info and perhaps the link to an engineering LibGuide. Make the handout visually appealing by including screenshots or images. In my handout, I include search tips and hints that lead students to the correct answers.

COOKING METHOD
1. Introduction
    a. Distribute the handout as students arrive. Begin the session by quickly introducing yourself. Since I'm the engineering liaison, I tell them a bit about my job, what I do, and how I can help them.
    b. Tell students they will be working on a group assignment with a number of problems that they will likely encounter during their engineering studies. Each group will decide for themselves how they want to tackle the assignment, but they only have a limited amount of time to finish.
    c. At the end of the allotted time, a member of each group will present their solution to one of the programs to the class, so all group members will need to know how to answer each question.
2. Group activity
    a. As the students are completing the assignment, walk around the classroom and be available to answer questions. I freely give hints if students are stumped, but I don't

outright give answers. With the handout, you will be able to see if students are struggling with any of the scenarios and offer advice.

   b. In each group, students become the teachers as they show their group-mates how they answered a question.

   c. As students finish the activity, approach those who have successfully answered a question and ask if they would present to the class. I pick one student from each group.

3. Presentations

   a. Have the selected students come up one at a time to the podium and demonstrate how they found the answer to a scenario. Oftentimes, students will have fun with the presentations and some do a thorough job explaining!

   b. Thank each presenter and then point out anything you wanted to cover that the student didn't mention. With this format, the students do most of the teaching, and you are adding content when necessary.

ALLERGY WARNINGS

When preparing this recipe, you may want to test out your scenarios on student assistants in your library. What seems clear to you may not be clear to them. When picking presenters, remind them that they need to know how they found their answer.

CHEF'S NOTE

In addition to engineering, I have used this approach in other subject areas when the course has no research assignment requirement. Rather than telling the students about all the resources and services the library has, I let them discover it for themselves. Students will be surprised with all you have to offer.

This Wine Tastes Like CRAAP!

Lee Ann Fullington, Health & Environmental Sciences Librarian, Brooklyn College—City University of New York, lafullington@ brooklyn.cuny.edu

NUTRITION INFORMATION

This recipe begins with a flipped model where students will have the CRAAP criteria (currency, relevance, authority, accuracy, and purpose) before they get to our happy hour, team-based learning lesson on evaluation of health information on the web. Many of us use the web to answer our own health and nutrition questions, just as the public health or nutrition students' future clients or community members will when they are in the field.

Public Health and Nutrition majors must take required introductory courses for these majors. These courses are perfect opportunities to introduce the concepts of health information literacy by having students encounter health information on the web and evaluate these sources using the CRAAP parameters.

NUMBERS SERVED

20–30 students

COOKING TIME

60–75 minutes

DIETARY GUIDELINES

This recipe introduces the students to the concept of "not everything you encounter on the web is credible," and in the health sciences and nutrition fields, where the students will be working with clients and communities to improve their health, finding and evaluating health information is critical.

ACRL FRAMEWORKS ADDRESSED

- Research as Inquiry
- Authority is Constructed and Contextual

MAIN INGREDIENTS

- ☐ Enough computers so students can be divided into small groups (3–5)
- ☐ Enough pre-selected websites so each group has one source to evaluate and report back on
- ☐ CRAAP worksheet (choose one that is an appropriate level for early college or late high school), and provide a copy to each student prior to the lesson to allow more time for group work and reporting back
- ☐ Poster-sized sticky notes and markers

MAIN COOKING TECHNIQUE

Flipped instruction, team-based learning, and CRAAP worksheet

PREPARATION

- ☐ Locate an appropriate reading level CRAAP worksheet or create your own based on one you find.
- ☐ Locate at least three different online sources to evaluate (one really questionable website, one news article that references a clinical trial or study, and one open access journal article for the clinical trial or study referred to in the news article). For this lesson, I chose an article that claimed, "Red Wine Makes You Skinnier" and found: sources from a website run by an anti-vaccination activist, who posted about red wine and weight loss; a local news story about red wine and weight loss that mentioned a clinical trial; an unintentionally funny *Daily Mail* article about drinking two bottles of wine and losing weight, complete with photos; and the scholarly open access article referenced by the news story.
- ☐ Create shortened URLs for each web source, or embed them into a Libguide so students have easy access.
- ☐ Share the CRAAP worksheet with the faculty member prior to the lesson, so students have a chance to read and think about the criteria and will (hopefully) be ready to dive into the group work without too much prior discussion. The discussion of the criteria will be embedded into the discussion with the groups when they report on the web source they were assigned.

COOKING METHOD

1. Give a brief overview of the session and ask the students if they read the CRAAP worksheet and if they have any questions.
2. Break the students into small groups and make sure each group has a computer.
3. Hand out hard copies of the CRAAP worksheet.
4. Give each group a large piece of paper or flipchart and markers so they can write down their own criteria and findings about the source they were assigned. Have them pick a recorder and a spokesperson, as they'll report back to the class with what they decide.
5. Assign each group a web source to evaluate and have them use the CRAAP parameters to do the evaluation.
6. Give them 10–15 minutes to discuss their source and the criteria. Ask them to note their thoughts on the large sticky notes in order to present them to the rest of the class.
7. Bring the class back together and have each group report on their assigned source. Use this time to discuss source evaluation and guide the discussion in such a way that the students will be able to understand and describe why a source is not as reliable or scholarly, and why a source is credible, etc.
8. As a wrap up, demonstrate a search in one of the library databases to introduce the idea of scholarly research and finding information using library sourc-

es. Demonstrating a government source such as *MedlinePlus* is also recommended, as another example of a great place to find reliable health information.

ALLERGY WARNINGS

Students may be shy and feel challenged to work in groups and work together, as this is a team-based learning approach to discussing health information literacy.

CHEF'S NOTE

Once the students warm up to their group members and start discussing what they are looking at, they tend to get into it and have fun picking apart the sources and find it empowering to use their new expertise in the discussion portion of the class.

The First Taste is Always with the Eyes:
Using Visual Cues to Teach Search Strategies

Christina E. Dent, Instruction Librarian, Emerson College, Christina_Dent@emerson.edu

NUTRITION INFORMATION
This recipe offers a visual way of teaching how to develop keywords and search strategies in order to find information. Students are shown an image and asked to use keywords to locate it using any search tool they choose. It is versatile in that the chef can choose to cover basic keyword/topic development concepts or they can introduce more advanced search concepts like Boolean logic—all through visualization. In addition, using images/screenshots from databases can demonstrate to students that not all information is freely available on the web.

NUMBERS SERVED
15–20 students

COOKING TIME
15 minutes or can be simmered for longer

DIETARY GUIDELINES
Through visualization, students learn how to create different keywords and strategies to find information.

ACRL FRAMEWORKS ADDRESSED
- Searching as Strategic Exploration
- Information Has Value

MAIN INGREDIENTS
- ☐ PowerPoint or other presentation software
- ☐ Images from the web and screenshots from databases
- ☐ Projector for instructor's station
- ☐ Computers/laptops that students will use

MAIN COOKING TECHNIQUE
Active learning, metacognition

PREPARATION
Fun and easy to make ahead! Ideally, the chef will choose a feature ingredient to unify the images used in the visualization. In this recipe, chefs chose images related to "Snowpocalypse" after a particularly brutal New England winter. Other featured ingredients have included: Godzilla, zombies, and sharknadoes.
1. Perform a web search to find images related to your featured ingredient. Google Images is a great tool for this. Find at least 2–3 images.
2. One image should be relatively easy to find—using the most basic keyword associated with your featured ingredient—and likely will come up as the first or second hit in a Google Images search.
3. Subsequent images should be progressively more challenging, requiring students to put keywords together or use Boolean operators or other advanced search techniques.
4. Final images should come from library databases, where the content cannot be accessed through a web search; students should either not find the image or hit a paywall. We used screenshots from ArtStor.
5. Using your presentation method of choice, set up images to display one at a time, moving from easiest to find to hardest to find.

COOKING METHOD
1. Challenge students to put their search skills to the test. Explain that they will be shown a series of images only and that they have to try and find the exact same image as quickly as possible using any search tool they like (spoiler: most will use Google). Tell students to raise their hands as soon as they find the image.
2. Project the first image; this should be the easiest one to find. For this recipe, we had simply searched "snowpocalypse" and chose the first image that came up in a Google Image search: a photograph taken during a blizzard.

3. Call out students as they raise their hands. Allow a few minutes for all students to try and find the image.

4. Call on the students who found the images first and ask them what they searched. Ask about keywords, the search tool chosen, any limiters used, etc.

5. Tell students that they are going to have a chance to practice again, and then show the next, more challenging image. For this recipe, we showed a photo image of the iconic "Make Way for Ducklings" statue covered in snow in the Boston Public Garden. Because students are only given the visual with no other clues, they need to test out different elements of the search. They need to first recognize that the image is of snow-covered duckling statues, then they need to focus on photographic images and filter out drawings or clipart images. Finally, they need to incorporate specifics into their search, such as the name of the statue or its location in Boston. For instance, a search for "ducklings in snow" will not be as fruitful as: snow "make way for ducklings" statue Boston.

6. Once again, have students raise their hands as they find the image. These searches should take longer as students try out different techniques. After several minutes, have students share which search terms they used. Have them discuss what worked and what didn't work. This conversation can easily segue into a quick demonstration of Boolean operators.

7. The final round of searching should incorporate an image from a database. In this case, we chose a screenshot from ArtStor featuring an oil painting by Albert Scott Cox entitled "Snowman." Students should have difficulty finding this; allow more time for this round to allow students to perform several searches, hopefully without success. When no students raise their hands, ask the class to shout out search terms they are trying. Ask them where they are searching for images. Most, if not all, will say Google or another search engine. Ask specifically if anyone is searching anywhere else. Reveal to students the source of the image and demonstrate how quickly you can find the exact image by searching "snowman" in ArtStor and limiting results to paintings only. This provides a great way to discuss not only developing useful keywords, but the importance of choosing the right information tool to perform the search.

ALLERGY WARNINGS

You may find that keywords that seem obviously connected to the image to you are not necessarily transparent to your students. For instance, when we based this activity on zombies, one of the more challenging images was a picture of a zombie librarian making a shushing gesture, with a book embedded in her skull. The visual elements of the image seemed obvious to us, but some students did not recognize the picture as embodying the concept of "librarian." Also, because this is a predominantly visual exercise, you'll want to be aware of your students' physical capabilities in advance. Check with the instructor beforehand to find out if anyone will require accommodation.

CHEF'S NOTE

We serve this dish up at the very beginning of our library workshops for first-year students. We're still surprised with how much students engage with this activity—you'll likely never hear such rapid-fire typing in another workshop setting! This recipe also works well to set the tone of a workshop and engage students' palettes for subsequent courses.

ADDITIONAL RESOURCES

Flickr's Creative Commons page has a wealth of free-to-use images: https://www.flickr.com/creativecommons.

From Potato Chips to Vegetables:
Embedded Instruction in a General Biology Classroom

Alyson Gamble, Science Librarian, New College of Florida & University of South Florida, agamble@ncf.edu; Tammera Race, Systems, Metadata & Assessment Librarian, New College of Florida & University of South Florida, trace@ncf.edu

NUTRITION INFORMATION

This instruction evolved from faculty-identified student needs: students struggled with finding and identifying scholarly resources. Initially offered as a one-shot session for a class, "From Potato Chips to Vegetables" developed into a flipped class using embedded librarians. Librarians partnered with faculty to help students develop a more sophisticated palate for research materials, with scholarly resource evaluation as a key nutrient. In this version of the recipe, the students engaged in a semester-long project contributing to a wiki on cancer research. However, the recipe can be adapted to courses in any discipline that include a research writing assignment.

NUMBERS SERVED

These activities can be offered to various class sizes.

COOKING TIME

- One 90-minute class session (can be varied)
- Preparation (3 hours)
- Evaluation (4 hours, depending on number of students)

DIETARY GUIDELINES

The overall learning outcome is that students will distinguish scholarly information from popular information in order to accurately identify appropriate resources for academic research. Additional outcomes may be identified as the students complete session activities.

ACRL FRAMEWORKS ADDRESSED

- Authority is Constructed and Contextual
- Information Creation as a Process
- Searching as Strategic Exploration

MAIN INGREDIENTS

- ☐ Two librarians
- ☐ One course faculty member
- ☐ Learning management system (LMS) access
- ☐ Article databases access
- ☐ A.S.P.E.C.T. checklist (Clark College Libraries; http://libraryguides.library.clark.edu/evaluating-information)
- ☐ Fake journal article (e.g., Alex Smolyanitsky's "'Fuzzy,' Homogenous Configurations") https://cdn2.voxcdn.com/uploads/chorus_asset/file/2522068/manuscript_%20Networking_Simpson.0.pdf

- ☐ Presentation creation software
- ☐ Video creation software
- ☐ Video hosting platform
- ☐ Laptops and Internet access for students

MAIN COOKING TECHNIQUE

Flipped classroom, incorporating opportunities for reflection and class discussion

PREPARATION

Prepare a short video (https://drive.google.com/file/d/0BxzNVUQ-BtRhdElDZGZNR3lG-WkU/view) highlighting the ingredients for a nutritious meal of scholarly research:

- Appetizers:
  - » Potato chips or vegetables (secondary or primary resources)
  - » A few yummy things or three crostini (qualitative or quantitative studies)
- Main course: Build your own salad (finding scholarly articles and quantitative studies)
  - » Library catalog
  - » Database metasearch
  - » Database subject search
  - » Google Scholar
- Dessert: Assorted berries (research management)

COOKING METHOD

1. As a course assignment, students choose a cancer research topic, develop a draft bibliography, and describe their process and rationale for choosing resources. Students post their sources and explanations to the LMS forum.

2. Before their class session, students watch the video and read the A.S.P.E.C.T. (Authority Sources Purpose Evenness Coverage Timeliness) Checklist for Evaluating Information (Clark College Libraries). Based on their new knowledge, students revise their resource lists and post the revised lists, with these considerations, to the discussion board:

   » Are your resources scholarly?
   » How do you know?
   » What would you still like to know about scholarly resources?

   Librarians review the students' posted answers, evaluate issues, and prioritize learning outcomes for the in-class session.

3. In class, librarians lead students in discussing their findings. Conversation begins with an open question about the appetizers and topics students would like to explore further. Discussion focuses on the differences between students' initial and revised searches.

4. With assistance from librarians, students work in small groups to locate and evaluate sources based on the A.S.P.E.C.T. Checklist. Each group reports about their experiences.

5. In addition to locating materials during this course, students review an article submitted to a predatory publisher. The article appears to be scholarly: it has authors, references, and figures. Upon inspection, the article proves to be bogus. Students discuss predatory publishers and analyzing articles based on content, not appearance.

6. After class, students are encouraged to ask questions of the librarians in person, via email, or through the LMS. The librarians provide feedback to students' forum posts about their sources.

ALLERGY WARNINGS

When giving feedback to students, be considerate of the students' vulnerabilities (e.g., embarrassment at being incorrect).

CHEF'S NOTE

This activity offers multiple assessment points: the pre-class activities on the discussion board, in-class reporting/discussion, and evaluation of the final wiki assignment. Discussion with the faculty members about student achievements before and after the exercise can assist with assessment.

ADDITIONAL RESOURCES

- From Potato Chips to Veggies: Finding Scholarly Resources: https://drive.google.com/a/ncf.edu/file/d/0BxzNVUQ-BtRhdEIDZGZNR3IG-WkU/view?pref=2&pli=1.

- Clark College Libraries: http://libraryguides.library.clark.edu/evaluating-information.

Blind Taste Test:
Helping First-Year STEM Students Understand "Information Creation as a Process"

Adrienne Button Harmer, Instruction Coordinator, Georgia Gwinnett College, harmer@ggc.edu; Bethany Havas, Reference & Instruction Librarian, Georgia Gwinnett College, bhavas@ggc.edu; Patti Lee, Head of Research Services, Georgia Gwinnett College, plee@ggc.edu; David Minchew, Reference & Instruction Librarian, Georgia Gwinnett College, dminchew@ggc.edu

NUTRITIONAL VALUE

We are finding that our first-year Chemistry students are able to find a lot of information online, but they can't differentiate or evaluate what they are finding. We get a lot of questions of the "how do I cite/use this website?" variety, when what they are looking at is a news article, a blog posting, an encyclopedia entry, a scholarly or trade or special interest group publication, a government brochure, or an actual website. What's worse, all of these are being valued the same in terms of cognitive authority, accuracy, and relevance. That's when we came up with our active learning in-class activity, the "Blind Taste Test."

In this activity, students are divided into groups and each group works to define an information product by its author, audience, and purpose. The groups report out to each other so that the entire class learns about the different creation processes of various information products, and how understanding the identifying characteristics of these processes and products can help students determine which information sources to use in their first-year STEM (science, technology, engineering, and mathematics) courses.

COOKING TIME

50–75 minutes

ACRL FRAMEWORKS ADDRESSED

- Information Creation as a Process
- Authority is Constructed and Contextual

COOKING TECHNIQUES

Small group work, structured jigsaw, peer-instruction with librarian facilitation

MAIN INGREDIENTS

- ☐ Marked stations around the instructional space, each clearly labeled with a specific type of information product. We use the large post-it sheets from a self-stick easel pad with the name of a type of information product written at the top (scholarly article, trade publication, news, magazine, etc.).
- ☐ Markers
- ☐ Small numbered post-its to designate groups
- ☐ List of pre-selected web links that can be made available to students. We tend to use class LibGuides to house the specified links. The "name" for each link is the appropriate group number (e.g. Group One, Group Two, etc.) so that students walk into each website blind.

☐ Salt and pepper: Internet-enabled devices and internet access. Our instructional space has 30 computers, but we often find students using their own devices to examine their assigned information product. It's also helpful if you are in a room with a projector, so that you can pull up the relevant web links as each group discusses and reports out to the entire class.

PREPARATION

You will need to spend a bit of time preparing for this activity. The most time-consuming part is selecting the information products that the students will be evaluating. It is helpful if the products are all linked to one another directly, and at the least they should be linked thematically and tied to the course content and relevant assignment or project.

Creating the marked stations and auxiliary materials is the least time-consuming aspect. Preparing a research guide for the course that includes the relevant web links and supporting material is recommended and will likely require a moderate time investment.

COOKING METHOD

1. Make introductory remarks emphasizing the context of why the students are in the library and the rationale for what they are about to do. Split the students into eight groups. Give each group a numbered post-it. Tell the groups to work together to look at the web link that corresponds to their group number (each link leads to a different type of information: scholarly, trade, news, magazine/entertainment, reference work, government, special interest group, and personal opinion/unsubstantiated). Direct students to work in their groups to discuss the typical author, audience, and purpose of their information product and to identify in which type of publication their information product is disseminated. When each group believes they know which type of information product they have, they are to stick their group post-it to the corresponding station marker. Once all groups have decided (or the allotted time is up), direct all the groups to go stand at the station they have chosen. (At this stage, typically, several groups of students may be standing in the wrong place, but we feel that's a learning opportunity for them, so we don't correct their efforts.)

2. Going in order from Group One to Group Eight, each group describes the underlying characteristics of the information product they have and the criteria they used to determine those characteristics. When the group seems to be at the "wrong" station, the library and chemistry faculty can solicit corrections from the other students or, if that is not forthcoming, can steer the group presenting into reconsidering. If all else fails, the faculty can point out why they think the students are in error and correct any misunderstandings. This is often a negotiable process and should be presented as a collective decision of the large group, not as a pronouncement handed down by the faculty. This continues until all groups have presented.

3. At the end of the instruction session, students are invited to leave comments at the ninth station (assessment) on more large pieces of paper. They are given markers and asked to leave at least one comment in at least one of four categories (I learned…, I'm still confused about…, This was useful because…, This would be better if…). The library faculty can collect these sheets and code the data to refine the activity in the future.

ALLERGY WARNINGS

- Students will complain at having to stand up and leave their devices behind for the reporting out, but they are much more engaged and participatory than when they are allowed to remain seated. Be prepared to make exceptions for those who are ill or infirm.

- Because this activity is directed at first-year students, these students may need to be encouraged to thoroughly skim their information products, but also need to realize they don't need to read and absorb the entire piece of information. They are looking for clues as to the author, audience, and purpose.

- Students can be hesitant to speak out during the reporting time, whether because they lack public speaking skills or because they fear being "wrong." It can be challenging to draw these students out.

- First-year students may find the activity challenging because they often want to know the "right" answer and don't realize that the usefulness of these information products is largely contextual.

- Pay attention to the pace and timing of the activity so that every group gets a chance to speak, but so that it also moves along quickly enough to keep the students engaged.

CHEF'S NOTES

We realized after our initial pilot that we needed to revise this to write the purpose of each information type on the station markers because consistently the first-year students put that the purpose of their type of information was "to inform."

The library faculty made new sheets with the type of information and its general purpose, which has helped these beginning students see that information can serve many different purposes (and also sometimes helps them figure out what type of information they have). For example, under scholarly articles, it says, "Purpose: to present (original) research that contributes to or advances knowledge in a field." If all of your selected information products are connected to one another, it can lead to a big "aha" moment for the first-year student.

For example, our unsubstantiated blog used a special interest group report as the basis for a blog post that went viral. Both our newspaper and magazine articles discussed the blog and its implications for food dye regulation and manufacturing (the topic of the chemistry course). The trade publication is about the regulation and manufacturing of the specific dye mentioned in the blog and subsequent popular press. The scholarly article presents research on the safety of that dye and the government brochure advises consumers of the results of that research. The reference source (Wikipedia) captures the debate on the safety of the dye, as well as providing factual information as to its chemical structure.

So, all eight of the information products are not only on the same topic (food dyes), but they actually are all part of the exact same conversation. It's a powerful moment in the class when those connections are made visible.

ADDITIONAL RESOURCES
Note: this activity was inspired by our reading of Troy Swanson's excellent article on

teaching students about cognitive authority: Swanson, T. (2005). Teaching students about information: Information literacy and cognitive authority. *Research strategies*, *20*(4), 322–333.

PART III. PROGRAMS

First Year Experience and Library Programming

Ready Player, Ready Research:
A Common Reader Caper

Jamie Addy, Instruction and Research Services Librarian, Georgia College, jamie.addy@gcsu.edu

NUTRITION INFORMATION

First-year students at Georgia College are expected to read a "common book" prior to arriving to campus for the Week of Welcome during the beginning of Fall semester. Ideally, the book serves as a touchstone for first-year students. Students are expected to discuss the book during Fall Convocation activities, prior to the start of the classes. The Ina Dillard Russell Library has been involved in many facets of the Common Reader program for several years and to varying degrees, including but not limited to: serving on the book selection committee, ordering and disseminating books on campus, and leading groups of students in book discussion circles.

One weakness of the Common Reader program at Georgia College is very little curricular integration of the book beyond the discussions that take place during Week of Welcome. This recipe was created to provide a fun and engaging outreach activity for first-year students while extending discussion of the text and highlighting library resources and services. The scavenger hunt activity was developed by librarians in the Instruction and Research Services Department for the 2014 Common Book selection, *Ready Player One* by Ernest Cline.

COOKING TIME

Varies. Our program took place over the course of three days. Activities within the program could be completed synchronously or asynchronously.

DIETARY GUIDELINES

- The recipe is designed primarily to extend discussions about the Common Reader and its themes through the lens of library resources and services.
- The recipe is also designed to quell library anxiety of new incoming students by promoting an atmosphere of fun in the library.
- Although the Common Reader program is geared toward first-year students, this outreach activity was open to any student who wished to participate.
- Successful completion of the activity requires nonlinear thinking and a variety of investigative methods.

ACRL FRAMEWORKS ADDRESSED

- Search as Strategic Exploration
- Research as Inquiry

MAIN INGREDIENTS

- ☐ Common Reader text/book
- ☐ Library databases or resources you wish to highlight

- ☐ Social media accounts (we used Facebook, Instagram, and Twitter)
- ☐ LibGuides and LibAnswers

PREPARATION

Librarians who read the book were invited to generate clues. Clues were also tested with willing library staff and student workers to make sure the clues were not too obscure or difficult. Because *Ready Player One* is suffused with pop culture and video game references from the 1980s, we were able to create fun, unexpected activities within the scavenger hunt, such as playing a video game for a high score on a vintage Nintendo game console (donated by a library staff member) in a library study room decorated to resemble a dorm room/basement hangout from the 1980s. We tried to create an atmosphere of playfulness that alluded to the book in ways that also highlighted library collections. For example, librarians in our Collection and Resource Services department worked with staff in Access Services to generate a display of DVDs/films referenced in the novel. We also created a large PacMan out of post-it notes and had other displays of 1980s memorabilia.

MAIN COOKING TECHNIQUE

1. Prep clues or activities that allude to your Common Reader text. Some of

our clues required students to physically explore an area of the library, while others highlighted library databases and relied on students using the appropriate keyword or phrase to access the next clue. Don't be afraid to get creative!

2. Enlist help of other librarians, library staff, or FYE program coordinators to test clues, activities, and otherwise support the hunt.

3. Set up or otherwise prepare social media accounts and LibApps (Springshare makes social media integration easy). In our activity, clues were released each day via our LibAnswers "Text a Librarian" service. We also used LibGuides to create and maintain a leaderboard (another allusion of *Ready Player One*).

4. Set dates for the activity and recruit students to participate. We put a "secret" starter clue in a box at our circulation desk prior to the official start of the scavenger hunt. Our student workers also recruited several friends to participate. Some instructors for First-Year Seminars offered students extra credit for participating in the activity.

5. Use social media to advertise, track, and support the activity. Participants were required to use the hashtag #gcready to document their scores and completion of activities.

6. Celebrate your winners! Our activity culminated in a pizza/cake party/'80s DJ party, where library staff and librarians dressed in their finest '80s attire and

FIGURE 1. PROMOTIONAL FLIER

announced the winners, along with the grand prize: a reserved study room for midterms and finals. Other participants were given parting gifts of library/Georgia College swag.

ALLERGY WARNINGS

As the "hunt" progresses, you may find students will drop out of the activity, especially if they see the leaderboard and perceive a lead as insurmountable. Using an assortment of clues and tasks within the hunt, so as to appeal to a variety of abilities and interests, will ease student drop-out.

CHEF'S NOTE

This type of activity may be best suited for a contemporary work of fiction. Although the activity we created was geared toward the first-year students by alluding to the Common Reader text, many upper-class students were driven to participate by the allure of the private study room during finals.

RPO - Clue 0001

In *Ready Player One*, Wade Watts shares a piece of dialogue from a John Hughes movie on page 62. Find the movie in the library. Flip over the DVD. There's a painting seen over a certain shoulder in a picture on the back.

Give the name of the painting to the Gatekeepers at the print desk as your pass key.

RPO - Clue 0003

Can you find the portrait of *Georgia State College for Women* president Dr. J. Luther Beeson in the library? Notice the artist's name. Receive the next clue by texting (478-845-3057) the name of the Georgia County where the artist grew up.

FIGURES 2 AND 3. EXAMPLES OF CLUE TEXTS

FIGURES 4 AND 5. SOCIAL MEDIA EXAMPLES

Superstition Speak Easy:
A Library First-Year Experience Event

Barbara E. Eshbach, Head Librarian, Penn State York, bee11@psu.edu

NUTRITION INFORMATION

Our small commuter campus does not have a formal First-Year Experience (FYE) program, so we developed ConnectED, a library FYE program, in order to provide opportunities for incoming students to connect with our campus community in a unique way. The five literacies (basic, information, civic and social, health, and financial) of PA Forward, a Pennsylvania Library Association initiative, form the foundation of ConnectED programs.

First-year students earn points (working toward winning a scholarship) for every event they attend, and additional points for each connection they make (either during events or on their own throughout the year). These connections are documented by having students fill out a "connection card."

We offer a variety of interactive, socially engaging, academic programs throughout the year, using several standard formats. This recipe is for a Speak Easy, which we describe as "an opportunity for conversation in a relaxed, informal setting for anyone who wants to improve their public speaking and learn something in the process."

COOKING TIME

50 minutes

DIETARY GUIDELINES

Research shows the importance of both academic success and social integration in terms of student persistence. While the library is most often thought of in terms of the academic support provided, we hope to also demonstate our value by offering events to socially engage our students and illustrate ACRL Framework concepts.

ACRL FRAMEWORKS ADDRESSED

- Research as Inquiry
- Scholarship as Conversation

MAIN INGREDIENTS

- ☐ A standard template to advertise and promote each event. This helps establish an identity and brand for your program and makes your advertising job easier.
- ☐ Interesting research articles to connect to your programs. These were a few of the articles we referred to during this event:
  - » Damisch, L., Stoberock, B., & Mussweiler, T. (2010). "Keep your fingers crossed! How superstition improves performance." *Psychological Science*, 21, 1014–1020. Ioi:10.1177/0956797610372631.
  - » Kramer, T., & Block, L. (2008). "Conscious and nonconscious components of superstitious beliefs in judgment and decision making." *Journal of Consumer Research*, 34, 783–793. doi:10.1086/523288.
  - » Zhang, Y., Risen, J.L., & Hosey, C. (2014). "Reversing one's fortune by pushing away bad luck." *Journal of Experimental Psychology: General*, 143, 1171–1184. doi:10.1037/a0034023.
- ☐ Refreshments
- ☐ Prizes. Our prizes for this event included a box of Lucky Charms cereal and the book *Good Luck of Right Now: A Novel* by Matthew Quick.
- ☐ Handouts
- ☐ Connection cards (if you would like to encourage and reward first-year students for making connections to others on campus).
- ☐ Evaluation forms

PREPARATION

Prepare a handout with relevant definitions (such as paraskevidekatriaphobia), interesting or controversial quotes from your research articles (to use to get the conversation started), and information about any upcoming library events. We included the following among the quotes on our handout: "Although superstitions are often culturally defined, the underlying psychological processes that give rise to them may be shared across cultures" (Zhang, Risen, & Hosey, 2014, p. 1183).

Find obscure superstitions and include the beginning phrase of each on the back of the handout to be used for the main activity.

MAIN COOKING TECHNIQUE

1. Hand out connection cards to first-year students, allowing time both at the beginning and the end of the session for them to make connections with other attendees.
2. Begin your conversation by asking if anyone had (or will have) a test that day and if they have any good-luck rituals associated with test taking.
3. While the handout includes interesting quotes to discuss, it helps if the group leader for this discussion has read all the articles and can keep the discussion going by providing other examples and questions to consider.
4. After your lively discussion, have everyone complete the sentences on the back of the handout.
5. Collect the handouts and play "Superstition Sentences" using the format and rules of the board game Balderdash. For example, our answers for the sentence, "If a bee enters your home, it's a sign you will soon have _____," ranged from "a baby" to "random women coming home" (which was probably

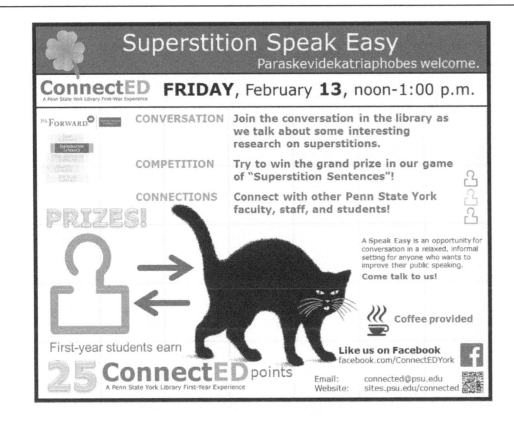

more wishful thinking than superstition). The actual answer, for which you have been awarded two points, was "visitor."

6. Total the points and award your prizes.
7. Have everyone complete an evaluation form.

ALLERGY WARNINGS
Don't be discouraged if your attendance is low—especially in the beginning of the semester. Word will get around that the library is having some interesting events and first-year students will appreciate the connections they make during these events.

CHEF'S NOTE
We are a small campus and our programs worked really well, even with limited participation as the small groups gave our first-year students the opportunity to make meaningful connections with all the other attendees. The evaluations for this program were excellent. Everyone who attended assigned a five (strongly agree) to the statement, "Today's program was enjoyable," with one attendee giving it a six! There was a lot of great interaction during this event and everyone enjoyed the game.

SUPERSTITION SENTENCES! Your name: _____

Write an ending for each of the following superstitions. The completed papers will be collected and each answer will be read, along with the correct answer. Players will then vote for the ending they think is the correct answer.

Scoring: A player gets 2 points for each vote their submission receives and an additional 2 points if they vote for the correct ending. If no player votes for the real ending, 3 points go into the bucket to be awarded randomly at the end.

1. An acorn at the window will
2. It's bad luck to put a hat on
3. Pictures of an elephant bring good luck, but only if
4. To dream of a lizard is a sign that you have
5. To protect yourself from witches, wear
6. Evil spirits can't harm you when you stand
7. It's bad luck to say the word "pig" while
8. A bed changed on Friday will
9. If someone is sweeping the floor and sweeps over your feet, you'll
10. To drop a comb while you are combing your hair is a sign of
11. If you catch a falling leaf on the first day of autumn. you will
12. It is bad luck to cut your fingernails
13. If a bee enters your home, it's a sign you will soon have a

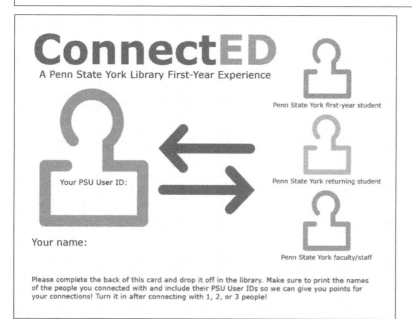

ConnectED
A Penn State York Library First-Year Experience

Penn State York first-year student

Penn State York returning student

Your PSU User ID:

Penn State York faculty/staff

Your name:

Please complete the back of this card and drop it off in the library. Make sure to print the names of the people you connected with and include their PSU User IDs so we can give you points for your connections! Turn it in after connecting with 1, 2, or 3 people!

I connected with_____
on _____ and discovered we had the
following in common:

Your PSU User ID:

Penn State York first-year student

I connected with_____
on _____ and discovered we had the
following in common:

Your PSU User ID:

Penn State York returning student

I connected with_____
on _____ and discovered we had the
following in common:

Your PSU User ID:

Penn State York faculty/staff

Who's the Boss?
Getting Students to Understand Authority in an Academic Context

Stephanie Gamble, Undergraduate Learning Specialist, University of Kansas, sgamble@ku.edu; Sofia Leung, Teaching and Learning Program Manager, Massachusetts Institute of Technology, sofial@mit.edu

NUTRITION INFORMATION

The University of Kansas (KU) Libraries partnered with the Office of First-Year Experience to provide a three-day lesson plan focused on the ACRL Framework "Authority is Constructed and Contextual" as part of University (UNIV) 101, a two-credit course to help first-year and transfer students transition smoothly to KU. Since 2012, the libraries provided each section of the course with an in-person research skills workshop. As part of the redesign of UNIV 101, librarians will no longer offer in-person workshops; rather, UNIV 101 instructors will be trained and given support materials to guide them through a libraries-developed lesson plan. This recipe is for an active learning game designed to reaffirm student comprehension of how authority is constructed and reaffirm engagement with different types of sources on the third day of the lesson.

COOKING TIME

50 minutes

DIETARY GUIDELINES

- Day one of the larger unit introduces students to source types with an information cycle activity, during which stu-

dents identify a source's attributes, type, and value in relation to a central event.

- The second day is a guided conversation in which students define authority and context within their own lives and correlate that to authority within academe. Students then evaluate sources they have brought in and determine the context for the source's authority.
- The final day is the Authority Game, which is meant to cement student comprehension of the concepts introduced previously. By the end of the unit, students will understand that different disciplines privilege different types of information for a variety of reasons. They will be able to evaluate source types depending on the context and be able to define and recognize different types of authority.
- The Authority Game is a collaborative, active learning game for play in class and can be adapted to classes of any size. To reinforce that authority is contextual, the game is played twice, once using an academic scenario and again with a non-academic scenario. The purpose of the game is to prompt a discussion among the students as to why certain source types are considered more authoritative and why.

- Through this active learning game, students are asked to consider the contextual authority of a range of source types while working with different information needs. In the game environment, students have the opportunity to work through the credibility of sources with their peers. As the game is being played, instructors will be able to informally assess whether students have achieved the learning outcomes set out for them.

ACRL FRAMEWORKS ADDRESSED

Authority is Constructed and Contextual

MAIN INGREDIENTS

- ☐ Please be aware of your classroom space and any students with mobility issues, as this game will require students to move around.
- ☐ Game pieces:
  - » Headbands (not required for alternative version, see Source cards)
  - » Source cards: one unique source card for each student in the class (alternative: can be replaced with sticky notes)
    - ○ The book, *Hard Choices* by Hillary Rodham Clinton
    - ○ An article from *The Atlantic*

entitled, "Can the Youth Vote Change Election Outcomes?" By Emily Richmond, public editor for the National Education Writers Association, (2/1/16)

- ○ U.S. Census Report on U.S. Population by Age and Sex (4/21/16)
- ○ A recording of one of the 2016 Presidential Debates
- ○ Your close friend or relative tells you who they're voting for
» Evaluation cards (listing author, audience, purpose, relevance, currency, context)
» Scenario cards: i.e. *Scenario 1 (academic)*: Write a research paper about how young people decide who to vote for in the 2016 elections; *Scenario 2 (non-academic)*: How do you decide whom to vote for?
» Authority indicators ("most authoritative," "least authoritative")

PREPARATION
☐ Create source cards, evaluation cards, scenario cards, and authority indicators
☐ Obtain headbands

MAIN COOKING TECHNIQUE
Before gameplay:
1. Each player takes a headband and a source card, unseen, to insert into the headband facing out.
2. Each player takes an evaluation card.
3. Players cannot tell other players what

source is on their card unless the player has guessed correctly.
4. Game facilitator places authority indicators on opposite sides of the room.

Gameplay:
1. Play begins once the facilitator has read a scenario from one of the scenario cards.
2. Once play begins, players can ask any other player a question to help identify the source on their head, using the evaluation cards. (Get out of your chairs!)
3. At any point a player may ask, "Am I a …?"
4. As a players learn about their source, arrange themselves where they think that source belongs in the room between "most authoritative" and "least authoritative."
5. Players can suggest rearrangement to any other players.
6. Play ends when all players arrive at a consensus as to their order or by time limit.

ALLERGY WARNINGS
- With the variety of sources used, there will be room for debate regarding the ordering of sources. Don't be afraid to encourage this discussion; it is a healthy part of the learning process.
- This may need to be reworked for students with disabilities (e.g. mobility or vision) to ensure that all students can participate.

DIY the FYE with Zines:
Two Mini Morsel Recipes

Erika Montenegro, Instruction and Outreach Librarian, East Los Angeles College, montene@elac.edu; Cynthia Mari Orozco, Librarian, East Los Angeles College, orozcocm@elac.edu

NUTRITION INFORMATION

Whether you're teaching your own first-year experience (FYE) class or a one-shot instruction session, we have a mini morsel zine recipe for you! The do-it-yourself (DIY) production and dissemination of zines make them a powerful tool for librarians teaching information literacy skills, especially in FYE programs. Here's how you can use them to DIY your college's FYE!

ACRL FRAMEWORKS ADDRESSED
- Authority is Constructed and Contextual
- Information Creation as Process
- Information Has Value
- Scholarship as Conversation

MAIN INGREDIENTS
- ☐ Paper (8½"×11")
- ☐ Collage material (e.g. magazines, newspapers, stickers, whatever you fancy!)
- ☐ Markers, pens, crayons, etc.
- ☐ Scissors and/or Exacto knife
- ☐ Glue
- ☐ Stapler (long-arm stapler, if possible)
- ☐ Access to computers or typewriters, copy machines, and printers

Zine Recipe 1: Using Zines in a Credit-Bearing FYE Class

NUTRITION INFORMATION

This mini morsel recipe is intended to show individual student growth over the course of a semester. Students create individual zines as their final project, which incorporate key elements from students' previous work, including weekly journals, vision boards, group discussions, papers, or presentations. They also include a section for students to reflect on short-term and long-term goals for personal student success, and a section for students to give advice to future incoming freshmen. Students learn the history and process of making zines as well as their role in scholarship and in the dissemination of information by contributing to a self-created FYE special collection of zines. Moreover, the zine project provides a natural outlet to bring in classroom discussions around copyright and fair use, citation practices, and open access.

PREPARATION AND COOKING TIME

Provide a clear description of your final zine project in your syllabus, as students will have many questions. Provide materials and references to facilitate your zine project in your course management system and/or through email correspondence, e.g. existing online tutorials and existing zine templates. There should be one class session dedicated to teaching zine-making, including 15–20 minutes of instruction, followed by in-class time to organize and begin building individual zines, as well as the opportunity for student questions. If your semester schedule permits, dedicate your last class session to zine presentations.

MAIN COOKING TECHNIQUE
1. The FYE course syllabus and final zine assignment
   a. Your credit-bearing FYE or library research course likely includes several assignments in alignment with your student learning outcomes. Incorporate elements from these assignments, as well as reflections on past assignments, into the final zine project, e.g. summary or reflection of weekly readings or reflection of processes. Each student will create their own zine.
   b. Additionally, include what you would normally assign as a final project or final paper (e.g. annotated bibliography).

c. Include a section in which students can provide tips and guidance to future first-year students for this class and the first year in general.

d. Include a required references section and/or criteria for citing materials used.

2. The zine workshop class
   a. Students learn the definition and history of zines.
   b. Students will learn how to assemble a zine. If possible, provide examples of zines that students can reference for formatting, design, and creativity.
   c. As students will likely be utilizing collage materials and remixing these for their zines, provide an overview on copyright and fair use that teaches students what they can use and how they can reuse these materials.
   d. Review the requirements for the final zine with the class.

3. Final presentations and zine collection (optional)
   a. Have students give a 5-minute presentation on their zine, their experience in the class, and what they have learned. Project the physical zines with a document reader or have students scan and submit PDF copies.

4. Creating the FYE zine collection
   a. Students donate and compile these zines to the library or FYE department to create a zine collection

about research skills and resources for new incoming FYE students. Of course, check with your library's Acquisitions Department or college's FYE coordinator for more specific directions.
   ○ Ideally, the collection will be housed in the FYE office where incoming freshman can view and borrow them.
   ○ The librarian can assist the students in coming up with a DIY circulation policy (if the students choose to have them borrowed).
   ○ Students can also opt to simply distribute copies during FYE recruitment events and keep an archive at the FYE office.

Zine Recipe 2: Outreaching and Teaching Using Zines for Instruction and/or Outreach Librarians

NUTRITION INFORMATION

This mini morsel recipe has instruction, outreach, and peer-to-peer teaching rolled up into one. Students develop public authorship and expertise with a hands-on activity, shape their knowledge based on the zine format, build on information by engaging with and understanding both open access and copyrighted materials, participate in a scholarly conversation within a peer-to-peer creative environment, and contribute to and care for a self-created FYE special collection of zines.

PREPARATION AND COOKING TIME

Prep and cooking time varies, since this involves instruction and outreach. Here are some general guidelines:
1. Collaborate with the FYE instructor on research orientation either face-to-face or online.
2. One instruction session.
3. One zine workshop. This is the most time-consuming part. The hands-on process is fun, but also takes a while. Give yourself at least an hour and half to two hours. Remember, you'll also help students figure out a circulation plan.
4. Any additional assistance needed in establishing the FYE zine collection.

MAIN COOKING TECHNIQUE

1. The one-shot instruction session
   a. Collaborate with the FYE instructor to tailor the research orientation to the class's assignment.
   b. Ask the instructor permission to offer a follow-up zine-making session, either during or outside of class. If the instructor needs some background on zines, feel free to simply share the zine description above. Ideally, it is easier to collaborate with the instructor early in the semester. Don't forget to invite the professor!
2. The zine workshop/research follow-up session
   a. Students learn the definition and history of zines.
   b. In small groups of two to three students:

○ Identify a research skill or library resource they learned about during the instruction session.
○ Create a zine that instructs and informs other new students about this skill and/or library resources.

3. Creating the FYE zine collection. See step 4 in the Main Cooking Technique section of Zine, Recipe 1.

ALLERGY WARNINGS

It is crucial to plan ahead of time with FYE instructors and coordinators. While it may seem like a lot of effort, especially if you have to sell FYE instructors or coordinators on the value of zines, this is where you get to flex your creative outreach skills. Trust me, your colleagues will be intrigued and start calling you the zine librarian.

CHEF'S NOTE

These zine mini morsels create an opportunity for improvisation and can be tailored to your needs. Make up your own rules and encourage your students to do the same. Also, think about using zines for collection development, publicizing services, general outreach, etc. There is a wealth of openly available information about zines online; for more information about zines, check out http://thepublicstudio. ca/images/diy/DIY-No2-Zines.pdf.

Special thanks to Art Center College of Design librarian Simone Fujita for immersing the authors in the zine experience!

The Perfect Fondue:
Partnering Advising and Libraries

Ashlyn H. Anderson, Director of Discovery Advising, Virginia Commonwealth University, ahanderson@vcu.edu; Donna E. Coghill, Community Engagement Librarian, Virginia Commonwealth University, decoghil@vcu.edu; Shajuana Isom-Payne, Director of Student Success, Virginia Commonwealth University, sipayne@vcu.edu

NUTRITION INFORMATION

Virginia Commonwealth University (VCU) fosters first-year student success through the use of various secret spices, including advising, tutoring, writing assistance, a common read program, and courses that introduce students to university academics. As co-chef, VCU Libraries offers services and resources designed to enhance the recipes provided by the First-Year Advisors. We take great pride in our excellent skills at melting advising and libraries into the perfect blend for every first-year palette.

VCU's First-Year Advisors have been in place since 2006, and have continually warmed and cultivated student success and engagement. VCU Libraries has simmered along with its Advising partner to create the perfect temperature to improve student retention. University Academic Advising and VCU Libraries have worked together to mix collaborative programming and online and on-site resources and materials to support the academic success, engagement, and retention of our first-year students.

COOKING TIME

Varies, depending on the resources available; general suggestion is the entirety of the first-year

DIETARY GUIDELINES

This recipe serves first-year students, their parents and families, and teaching faculty, by linking high-impact practice to retention through the implementation of an innovative student-centered environment and engagement.

MAIN INGREDIENTS

☐ For this recipe, librarians will need to have on hand a willing academic advising partner and a first-year student population.

☐ Additional ingredients may vary, including online library guides such as LibGuides (guides.library.vcu.edu/univ101, guides.library.vcu.edu/univ102, guides.library.vcu.edu/univ103), and specialized collections geared to student success, time management, study skills, and major and career exploration.

PREPARATION

Before beginning this recipe, you should carefully select your cheeses. We find that the best cheeses for this fondue are those to which you are already familiar—your strongest allies in Advising are those with whom you may already have developed a

relationship. Look to those who you have worked with in other capacities, creating LibGuides, workshops, and New Student Orientation partners, to name a few.

Another method of successful cheese selection includes winning over administrators:

☐ Identify stakeholders.
☐ Identify ways it supports retention and student engagement.
☐ Expand research opportunities for publications.
☐ Identify how this supports the university's mission.

The best fondue starts with the best pairing—familiar faces working together!

MAIN COOKING TECHNIQUE

1. Find a good partner. Each recipe works in a unique way; the best way to start is with someone with whom you already have a good working relationship.
2. Identify immediate needs and opportunity for collaborative effort(s).
3. Start small—one or two cheeses is all you need to start your fondue. Remember, piloting programming is a great way to test your team cooking skills.

4. Meet regularly to review and assess effective (and tasty) recipes (programs). Repeat at least once per semester.
5. Experiment with more exotic cheeses as your comfort level with your new Fondue Partnership grows.

ALLERGY WARNINGS

- Allergy warnings may include debunking the myth of the helicopter parent and empowering faculty to see parents as partners.
- An important note: This partnership does not require additional financial resources, a common misconception regarding new program development. Cheese does not have to be expensive.

CHEF'S NOTE

With this recipe, readers will be able to develop a deeper understanding and recognition of the interdisciplinary nature of the collaborative partnership between advisors and librarians. Below are our favorite recipe variations:

- First-Year Experience Curriculum Committee: librarian participates in setting curriculum for UNIV 101 and UNIV 102 classes; core classes that support FY student retention and academic success.
- The library has a curated collection of books and DVDs focused on study skills, time management, goal setting, leadership, and critical thinking. Included in this collection is an extensive career and academic program collection to assist students in finding the right major.

- Focused physical spaces within the library, encouraging students to utilize the library as a meeting and group project/brainstorming place.
- Librarian attending advising faculty trainings, book selections, and other opportunities.
- Advisors attending library trainings, database overviews, and collection reviews.
- Collaborative meetings, working together to solve common problems and issues for FY students.
- Using parents as partners in education, including online resources, parent classes, and engagement in orientation activities.

SELECTED BIBLIOGRAPHY

- Bean, John P. "College Student Retention." Ed. James W. Guthrie . *Encyclopedia of Education*. 2nd ed. Vol. 1. New York: Macmillan Reference USA, 2003. 401–407.
- Bell, Steven. "Keeping Them Enrolled: How Academic Libraries Contribute to Student Retention." *Library Issues* 29.1 (2008).
- Blackburn, Heidi. "Shhh! No Talking about Retention in the Library!" *Education Libraries* (2010): 24–30. *Information Literacy Competency Standards for Higher Education*. Rep. Chicago: Association of College & Research Libraries, a division of the American Library Association, 2000.
- Mezick, Elizabeth M. "Return on Investment: Libraries and Student Retention." *The Journal of Academic Librarianship* 33.5 (2007): 561–66.
- Nutt, Charlie L. "Advising and Student Retention and Persistence." *Advising and Retention*. NACADA. Web. 18 Feb. 2016.
- Oakleaf, Megan, Phd. *The Value of Academic Libraries, a comprehensive Research Review and Report*. Rep. Chicago: Association of College and Research Libraries. 2010.
- Stoller, Eric. "5 Ways to Grow Your Digital Fluency." *Inside Higher Ed*. 4 Dec. 2014.

Cooking with the STARs (Science, Technology, & Research) Early College High School Program

Matthew Harrick, Outreach & Instruction Librarian, Brooklyn College—CUNY, mharrick@brooklyn.cuny.edu

NUTRITION INFORMATION

Preparing early college high school freshman for college-level research through intense preparation for college is one of the driving goals of the Early College High School Initiative (ECHS), an initiative that partners high schools and colleges/universities to prepare high school students for higher education. If your institution has an ECHS partnership, or if you provide outreach to local high schools, this program can help to ease the high school to college transition by working with high school students at the beginning of their high school career, as opposed to the end (typically their senior year).

This program gradually introduces high school freshmen to library resources and information literacy skills through a structured project in an effort to prepare them for college-level research in their junior and senior years of high school, and as they make the transition to first-year students at colleges and universities.

COOKING TIME

20 hours prep time (writing the curriculum, coordinating with other units, putting materials together). Total duration: 6 90-minute sessions over 6 weeks (one per week): 9 hours. Serves: 2–15 students.

DIETARY GUIDELINES

- This program lays a solid foundation of research skills and "library comfort" for high school freshmen in a fun, un-graded (therefore relatively informal) way.
- These skills will work to the students' advantages when they return as juniors and seniors enrolled in credit-bearing courses, and will benefit them when they move on to full-time college/university status.
- Working so closely with a partnering ECHS demonstrates a deep commitment to college readiness on the part of the collaborating academic library.

MAIN INGREDIENTS

- ☐ Classroom with computers for each student
- ☐ Folder including blank paper, weekly worksheet, library locations bookmark, borrowing form/card
- ☐ Librarian
- ☐ Archivist (or special collections librarian)
- ☐ High school teacher chaperone
- ☐ Illustration materials (pencils, markers, etc.)
- ☐ Student emails
- ☐ ACRL Information Literacy Thresholds, Common Core State Standards, to taste

PREPARATION

- ☐ Coordinate with the ECHS program director to let them know you're offering the program, where it takes place in the library, and what the students will work on.
- ☐ Coordinate with the archivist to schedule a visit to Special Collections; pre-select primary sources for visit.
- ☐ Coordinate with Access Services to arrange for borrowing privileges, get borrowing forms and cards, choose expiration date, etc.
- ☐ Write weekly lesson plans.
- ☐ Write a 6-week worksheet for students.

MAIN COOKING TECHNIQUE

1. Week 1: Orient your group to the library's services/resources with a colorful presentation featuring images from around the library. Discuss the syllabus and weekly worksheets and detail expectations of the seminar. Move on to a basic discussion about research itself, and then have the group "illustrate" their conceptions of how they do research using markers, colored pencils, and other supplies. Finally, discuss the seminar's science-related topic (for example, the environment).

2. Week 2: This week, focus on books. Narrow topics, discuss keywords/phrases and then have the group fill out the worksheet with their own keywords/phrases. Demonstrate how to use the catalog and how to use basic Boolean searching skills. Once they've found a book in the catalog, have them fill out their borrowing forms, get their library cards, and find and check out their books. Discuss APA (or another citation style) and then have each student create a citation for their book on their worksheet. Each following week will have students create citations for the different sources they find.

3. Week 3: In this session, move on to database searching to build on the skills laid down in week 2. Discuss the difference between popular/scholarly sources. Then, demonstrate a general database and have the group find one of each type of article.

4. Week 4: This week, you'll visit Special Collections for a presentation by the archivist, who will have primary sources pre-selected and waiting for the group to investigate.

5. Week 5: In week 5, discuss and demonstrate differently formatted resources, such as videos, blogs, and zines.

6. Week 6: Final presentations: Have the group create new illustrations that show what they think of research after learning about it and practicing it for 6 weeks, and compare with their original illustrations. Each student can get in front of the group to share what they've learned, what their favorite type of source is, etc.

ALLERGY WARNINGS

- It can be tricky to keep high school freshmen interested for 90 minutes, especially at 9 a.m. on Friday mornings. It helps having a good relationship with their chaperone, who can help to keep them on track and off of social media or online gaming sites.
- Don't forget they've checked out books. Make sure they renew or return on time!

CHEF'S NOTE

For a more interactive experience, allow the students to pick their topics. Remind them they do research all the time online, and that what they do in this seminar (and in future coursework) will build on the skills they already have.

Serving Those Who Served:
Outreach for Student Veterans

Nancy Fawley, Director of Information and Instruction Services, University of Vermont, nfawley@uvm.edu

NUTRITION INFORMATION

The generous benefits of the Post-9/11 Educational Assistance Program have encouraged many veterans to seek a college education. Colleges and universities are seeing an uptick in veteran enrollment. For librarians wishing to support student veterans, it is important to understand the unique needs of veterans transitioning from military life to civilian life as students before stepping into the kitchen. Veterans are transitioning from a highly structured and interdependent environment to one where individuality and inquisitiveness are encouraged and expected.

These are typically non-traditional students: some are older; some may or may not have prior college experience; some, especially female veterans, may be single parents. They are also a diverse group. Some may have seen combat while others may have had office jobs. Many have lived and served overseas and have developed a broader global perspective. Military service emphasizes trust and teamwork, which develops leadership and initiative. Student veterans take this spirit of persistence and sense of duty with them into the classroom.

COOKING TIME

Cooking time will vary, but should include outreach to the student veteran's office in addition to teaching a workshop.

DIETARY GUIDELINES

* This recipe is a combination of co-curricular outreach and course instruction that aligns with universities' efforts to support veteran students and ensure their success.

MAIN INGREDIENTS

☐ Resource Guide with links to key library resources, information on getting help from a librarian, and web resources for veterans
☐ Library handouts, such as quick tips for various citation styles
☐ Flyer of upcoming library workshops
☐ Giveaways, if available; the best include a URL to contact a librarian
☐ Business cards to share with the students

PREPARATION

Reach out to the department on campus that oversees veteran students. The staff in these offices wants their students to succeed and welcomes programs that will support student success. Many student

veteran offices offer presentations for faculty on understanding the student veteran population. Attend one, if possible, before you start cooking. They will help foster an understanding of the experiences of student veterans. Many of these types of presentations include information that will help build awareness of individuals who have experienced trauma.

MAIN COOKING TECHNIQUE

1. Working with the student veteran office on your campus, develop a workshop that highlights library services. The challenge is that it is not instruction tied to an assignment. Instead, aim to find a topic that is relevant to student veterans, such as a "getting started" introduction to research and an overview of library services, such as borrowing privileges, librarian assistance, and interlibrary loan.
2. Introduce yourself as the liaison to the student veteran office. If you have served in the military or lived overseas, you could share that information with the group to build a rapport.
3. Military service fosters the development of teamwork and initiative. Play to the students' strengths and include group work and goal-oriented active learning.

4. Introduce the research guide for veteran students and highlight the tabs for library resources, websites for veterans' services, and ways to get help from a librarian.
5. Be sure to promote self-service virtual reference and research tutorials, if offered at your library.
6. Distribute your business cards and stress that you are their personal contact in the library.
7. Distribute flyers for library workshops, upcoming events, and other information.

ALLERGY WARNINGS

Respect that some veterans prefer not to discuss their military experience in class. A better approach is to acknowledge their veteran status, but treat them as the student population.

CHEF'S NOTE

Separate personal feelings about military and war from the professional obligation to foster scholarly inquiry and student success.

Nothing Beats Home Cooking!
Programming for First-Year International Students
Joi Jackson, Online Learning Library Specialist, George Mason University, jjackso4@gmu.edu

NUTRITION INFORMATION
This recipe introduces international students to the library's website and resources. This event is easily customized to your budget, space, equipment, personnel, time constraints, and technological savvy. It can also be adapted for online students.

COOKING TIME
50–60 minutes

DIETARY GUIDELINES
This recipe is intended as outreach to hard-to-reach student populations, specifically international students and online students. Particularly, international students will "understand how information systems… are organized in order to access relevant information."

MAIN INGREDIENTS
- [ ] 20 questions based on foreign popular media (K-pop, J-pop, Bollywood, KDrama, Telenovelas, etc.)
- [ ] Answer Sheets
- [ ] 5–10 library quiz questions/answers
- [ ] 20 tie-breaker questions
- [ ] Computer
- [ ] Projector
- [ ] Sign-in sheet (includes name and e-mail address)
- [ ] Assistant(s)
- [ ] Follow-up survey
- [ ] Place to showcase library resources related to quiz topic (books, DVDs, CDs) (optional)
- [ ] Food (optional)
- [ ] Prizes (optional)

PREPARATION
Select questions/answers, develop presentation, secure event venue, fund and purchase food and/or prizes (optional), and solicit assistant(s). Implement your marketing strategy at least two weeks in advance.

MAIN COOKING TECHNIQUE
1. The librarian and assistant(s) have students sign in. Each student is then given an answer sheet.
2. Library website introduction—10 minutes. The librarian gives a tour of the library's website. The goal is to give a "top 5–10 things you need to know" presentation on the website; for example, where to find books, articles, and media, how to contact a librarian, finding their library account and how to login, etc. If possible, include a database that has more resources on the pop culture topic. For instance, for a K-pop quiz, show students how to access a music database that has additional K-pop songs.
3. Library quiz—5 minutes. The librarian gives a short quiz based on the website introduction. Award bonus points to the student's answer sheet for each correct response.
4. Pop culture quiz—15 minutes. The librarian administers the quiz to the students. The quiz could require students to: "name that tune" after hearing short sounds clips; "name that band," based on demonstrations of dance moves; traditional trivia questions; etc.
5. Determine winners—10–20 minutes. The librarian and the assistant(s) collect the answer sheets and determine the winners. During the grading, students can mingle, eat and drink. If there is a tie, have students answer the tiebreaker questions.
6. Review answers—10 minutes. The librarian reviews the answers with the students. Showing short clips of the music video, film, etc. will provide clarification for students with incorrect answers.
7. Follow-up—Using the information from the sign-in sheet, send a survey to all of the participants. The survey should gauge what they learned about the library and ask for feedback on the event.

ALLERGY WARNINGS
Be prepared for excited students! This is intended to be fun and a bit loud, so make sure you choose a space that won't disturb others. Also, be prepared to use your best "shh!" so that everyone gets a chance to participate and to keep the event on schedule.

CHEF'S NOTE
- The excitement of the students is contagious. If you can, take pictures and/or video; it is great for marketing. Students may start singing and dancing!
- A hybrid presentation of the event is also possible. Simply present the questions in person and online through online collaboration or polling software.
- For a hybrid presentation, it is helpful if the prizes are digital (e.g. gift cards). For example, with gift cards, you can print out the codes for winners in person or send them to the online winners via e-mail.
- Marketing is crucial. If you can, place an advertisement in the content management system. I had my best attendance with this method. Also, partnering with international student organizations and university departments is a great way to get funding and share information with students.
- Another great benefit of this event is that it attracts local students as well.

College Bookworms:
Leisure Book Clubs in Academic Libraries

Charissa Powell, Undergraduate Experience Librarian, Kansas State University, powellc@ksu.edu

NUTRITION INFORMATION

Starting a book club for college students can be daunting. With the proper planning you, too, can start one on your campus. This book club was created purely by student interest and demand. Multiple students had inquired about whether or not there was a book club on campus and until now there was not one. This program will be helpful because it provides students a way to get involved on campus, an outlet to talk about something they have love, and a personal way of getting to know a librarian.

COOKING TIME

This particular program is on-going during the academic year. How often the book club meets is flexible and up to the librarian. How often the book club meets is flexible; the club could meet once a month, every other week, every week, etc. The cook time could be adjusted to the needs of the librarian—this could also be done during just the fall semester in accordance with a common read program.

DIETARY GUIDELINES

- The book club supports leisure reading and discussion among college students, who might not have an outlet for this on their own.

- Having a book club serves as an outlet for library marketing and outreach. This book club meets in the library, so it gets a group of students walking through the library doors at least twice a month.
- Students participate by selecting books and planning discussion sessions.

ACRL FRAMEWORK ADDRESSED

- Scholarship as Conversation

MAIN INGREDIENTS

- ☐ Meeting space (a room with enough chairs for book club members)
- ☐ Flier for book club meetings
- ☐ Group of students who love to read and want to talk about it

PREPARATION

- ☐ Advertise for a book club interest meeting. Some ideas for advertising locations: fliers at service points inside the library, announcement e-mail to various campus list-servs, and the English Department bulletin board (maybe a little stereotypical, but it worked well).
- ☐ Create/decide on a mode for staying in communication with students, such as Facebook group, list-serv, etc.

MAIN COOKING TECHNIQUE

1. Find a group of students who love reading. You might find these students are already at the library.
2. Get those students together for book club meetings.
3. Select a book to read as a group. Make sure the students are part of this process.
4. Have a discussion about that book, facilitated by one of the students.
5. Pick the next book. Consume and repeat!

ALLERGY WARNINGS

- Advertising and recruitment. Both are important so that students are aware of the book club and show up for meetings.
- Meeting day/time. Ask students what is convenient for them and keep that a set meeting for the semester.
- If you have a budget, you can buy a book for each student. If your budget does not allow for this, there are other options, such as discussing the campus common read book.

CHEF'S NOTE

- This book club has been a huge source of professional satisfaction and happiness. I did not set out to create this program; it evolved organically by way of student interest.

- It was a little slow getting the book club started. There were several meetings where we just discussed what we wanted this book club to be. This was important to me because I wanted to make sure that the book club was meeting the students' needs.

- Advice: Let the students take some ownership and leadership in this program!

Locally Sourced Materials:
Primary Sources Pulled from the Archival Garden

Erin Passehl-Stoddart, Head, Special Collections and Archives, University of Idaho, estoddart@uidaho.edu

NUTRITION INFORMATION

Special Collections and Archives was invited to host two introductory English courses comprised mostly of first-year students. We hosted the classes for one week and met three times for approximately 50 minutes each. The first session was an introduction to archives; the second session was a hands-on activity that included individual and group work that examined primary sources; and the third session introduced students to digitized primary sources. For most students, this was their first experience with archives and, for many, the university library at large. After each session, students wrote blog posts answering specific questions that targeted their experience.

We try to introduce students to primary source research, much like disguising vegetables in a casserole, to make it as interesting and current to their lives as possible. These sessions are also a great opportunity to expose students to new perspectives they may not have experienced (Greek life, LGBTQA, veterans, etc.). Students will take away an awareness of how to analyze primary sources and an introduction to artifactual and digital literacy. This recipe supports student engagement and retention by introducing students to local history and provides sustenance for their college years ahead. These archival sessions could

be transferred to other lower- or upper-level courses on campus, and the writing assignment is easily scaled into a short individual or group paper or presentation.

COOKING TIME

Two or three 50-minute sessions over the course of one week. This could be adapted to one hands-on session, if needed due to time or class restraints, as outlined below. Serves class sizes of 10–30 students working in groups of 3–5 people to ensure participation from all students.

DIETARY GUIDELINES

- This recipe serves to connect undergraduate students to primary source research, be exposed to archival literacy, and continue on a path of lifelong learning in libraries. This recipe connects new students to non-traditional library sources, such as university archives.
- This is an excellent way for archives and special collections to reach out to undergraduate students and instructors in general education courses. A further suggested reading is *Using Primary Sources: Hands-On Instructional Exercises* by Anne Bahde, Heather Smedberg, and Mattie Taormina, 2014.

ACRL FRAMEWORKS ADDRESSED

- Authority is Constructed and Contextual
- Research as Inquiry
- Scholarship as Conversation
- Searching as Strategic Exploration

MAIN INGREDIENTS

☐ Archival collections that document the history of the college/university encompassing multiple formats (photographs, publications, scrapbooks, media, etc.). The collections should be theme- or topic-based for each table. Our themes included athletics, Greek and student life, and campus technologies.

☐ Room with tables so that students can work in groups and spread out archival materials. It can literally be any room; our instruction labs were booked, so we met in the library staff lounge.

PREPARATION

☐ Have the archivist and class instructor meet to develop learning objectives. Ours included: students being exposed to archival materials and research; learning how to analyze primary sources; and how to evaluate information.

☐ Decide on table themes in advance. We allowed students to vote for their top three choices in a poll before the hands-on activity took place (optional).

☐ Pull archival materials on the selected topics, taking care to include multiple formats and different perspectives. Include nutritious sources such as student newspapers and yearbooks.

☐ Pull secondary sources on the same topics for comparison, such as published campus histories.

☐ Write questions to assist students with analyzing primary sources and print out for use during the hands-on activity.

☐ Set out documents and artifacts by theme at tables in advance to save class time. A placard may note the theme for students to choose from.

MAIN COOKING TECHNIQUE

1. Main course: Hands-on activity using university archives (approximately 50 minutes)
   a. Divide students into groups of four or five at a table. Each student should have archival materials to analyze with a common table theme. Our final themes included athletics (men, women, and intramural), Greek life, student life, and "old school technology," i.e. campus radio and television stations.
   b. Individual work (15 minutes). Have students examine their particular document/artifact for a few minutes on their own. Students may use the printed out questions to assist with analyzing the document: Describe

what you see. Who created these materials? What was the original use of this material? Why do you think this item is important? What is left unanswered? What is a potential research question that you could answer using these materials? How would secondary sources help provide answers?

   c. Group discussion at tables (10–15 minutes)
      ○ Encourage students to talk among themselves to identify similarities and differences in the documents. How do different materials relate to the common table theme?
      ○ Introduce general primary and secondary sources to be used and analyzed by the entire class; examples include yearbooks, campus newspaper, and books written about campus history.

   d. Groups report out to class (20 minutes)
      ○ Ask at least one student from each group to describe his or her documents to the rest of the class. Have the student answer one or two of the questions posed depending on time available.
      ○ As a class, leave time to discuss how the primary sources provide evidence and information of a particular event, student group, etc.

   e. Individual written analysis (blog posts). Since locally sourced "food" does not come with nutrition labels, the written responses incorporate nutrition into the information diet:
      ○ Describe something you saw today when we visited the archives. What was it? What was notable about it? Why did it interest you? What inferences can you make or what questions does it raise?
      ○ Think about your family or your hometown. If there were archives dedicated to your town or family, what would they contain? Why?
      ○ What sort of things do you think are relevant primary sources in your own life? What kinds of primary sources do you use?
      ○ What new questions do you have after today? Your questions can be about the archives or about specific things you saw.
      ○ Do you notice any similarities or differences when you compare the archive source with a similar source today? (For example, a yearbook or newspaper then vs. a yearbook or newspaper now?)
      ○ Did any of the sources you handled confirm or disprove any of your preconceived notions? Explain.

ALLERGY WARNINGS

- Planning table themes in advance allows students to have more buy-in to the hands-on activity and makes it easier for the instructor to design questions in advance.
- The instructor should be prepared to handle questions about historical names, terminology, and events depicted. This activity has the potential to include materials or questions that do not always promote proud behaviors or events on campus. These topics can lead to in-depth discussions related to research topics and show how history can inform current societal issues.
- Some students may need assistance with document analysis; be prepared to keep students focused on the group questions they should answer.
- Students may vary in their enthusiasm to work in groups. Students could alternatively work in pairs at the table and then discuss the questions as a group. The instructor should visit each table and check on the student's progress at least once while they are working; this allows for questions to be posed that some students do not want to ask in front of the entire class.
- Provide adequate time for students to work individually and collaboratively. In my experience, as students examine their primary source documents, the more interested they become in the topic or want to examine it further. Make sure to leave time for this to happen before reporting out in groups.

CHEF'S NOTE

Additional food courses or alternative cooking techniques can be introduced, depending on the amount of time available. An hors d'oeuvres serving could include an archives tour to show off the garden where the "food" was pulled from. Dessert could include a presentation on digitized primary sources, including institution-specific digital collections. Small slips of paper asking why archives matter allows students to feed their imagination and open them up to new experiences in the classroom.

These sessions were designed to act as a quick introduction to archives and to get students interested in campus history and consider how they might use primary sources in their classes. These classes included student athletes and students involved with the Greek system on campus; many connected directly to their fraternity history or looked at how their particular sport has evolved on campus. Some students took selfies with their favorite archival material. Tables that include multiple formats on one topic allowed for a broader discussion of how resources relate and connect to each other. The introduction of secondary sources on each topic helped students to differentiate between those and primary sources. The writing exercises (blog posts) allowed students to worked well to record their thoughts. It would be nice to incorporate this into a larger assignment in the class (paper, presentation, etc.).

Cooking on High with Early College & Dual-Enrollment Programs

Jolene Cole, Instruction Coordinator & Associate Librarian, Georgia College, jolene.cole@gcsu.edu

NUTRITION INFORMATION

Many academic libraries serve populations beyond traditional students, faculty, and staff. Early College and dual-enrollment programs are among the many high school-level programs offered at universities across the country. Librarians should recognize that these students might not be able to fathom how the library could benefit them. They may not even realize the library is something that is theirs to explore and use. By creating engaging and interactive programming, librarians not only welcome these students to campus, but also encourage students to utilize the library's services. If libraries learn to connect with these students early on, the more likely they are to use the library later on in their college careers.

NUMBERS SERVED

10–70+ students

COOKING TIME

50 minutes

DIETARY GUIDELINES

- This activity fosters relationships with high school programs that utilize the campus library by introducing the academic library in a creative and non-threatening environment. Librarians are encouraged to build strong partnerships with the programs' administrators.

- This allows the two groups time to establish a set of mutual outcomes and conduct the orientation yearly for incoming students. The joint program encourages students to make connections with librarians beyond the traditional one-shot or class assignment.

ACRL FRAMEWORKS ADDRESSED

Students will cook with the Framework areas Search as Strategic Exploration and Information Creation as a Process by finding needed information and acknowledging that information can be communicated in a range of formats.

MAIN COOKING TECHNIQUE

The instructor opens with a short cooking demonstration by informing student chefs how to create recipe cards. Student chefs are then broken into groups of 4 or 5, depending on the size of the group. Chefs then return to the kitchen to share the recipe cards they have created by exploring the library.

MAIN INGREDIENTS

- ☐ LibGuide to store the recipe cards
- ☐ Padlet.com or a similar program for creation of student recipe cards
- ☐ Tablets, such as the iPad, for each group of student chefs
- ☐ A worksheet full of prompts for students to answer as they create their recipe cards
- ☐ Wi-Fi and an instructor station with projector
- ☐ A map of the library (optional)

PREPARATION

1. The librarian or head cook should prep the kitchen by creating a LibGuide that will be home to each recipe card the student chefs create. A welcome tab to introduce students to the process can be helpful, followed by a tab for each group of chefs.
2. Librarians will then need to add a Padlet page to each tab so that the student chefs can create their own cards using prompts given to them via the worksheet.
3. The worksheet will include the following prompts:
   - » Snap a pic of the desk where you check out books.
   - » Snap a pic where you can get help with your research.
   - » Snap a pic of something that you didn't know the library had.
   - » Find a book that has the first half of its call number QC 981 and grab a pic.
   - » Snap a picture of the weirdest book you can find in the reference section.

» Snap a pic of something that you find confusing.
» Locate the service area where you can get extra help from tutors. Take a pic.
» Locate a library service, e.g. writing center, laminating, printing, computers, etc. Take a pic.

MAIN COOKING TECHNIQUE

1. Welcome student chefs with a brief introduction to the library.
2. Separate the chefs into groups of 4–5, depending on the number of students. Assign each group a tab in the LibGuide.
3. Using the welcome tab of the LibGuide, explain the steps to create their own Padlet page.
4. Student chefs will be set free to explore the library by snapping pictures of the various ingredients that they need to find to create their recipe card. Allow the students about 20 minutes to engage with the front of the house, library, and library services.
5. Student chefs will return to the kitchen and present their recipe cards to the class. Allow approximately 10–15 minutes for this section.
6. For dessert, wrap up the program with a simple assessment of your choice.

ALLERGY WARNINGS

If you find the chefs aren't cooking to their abilities, you may want to encourage them with prizes and add a little competition to the activities.

CHEF'S NOTE

- Student chefs may need a small amount of assistance in using the technology.
- This activity requires reliable Wi-Fi access.
- This activity can also be adjusted to work with incoming first-year students.

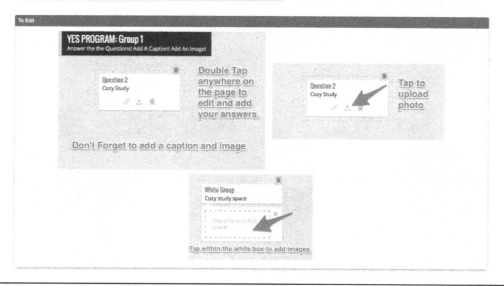

B. Library Programming

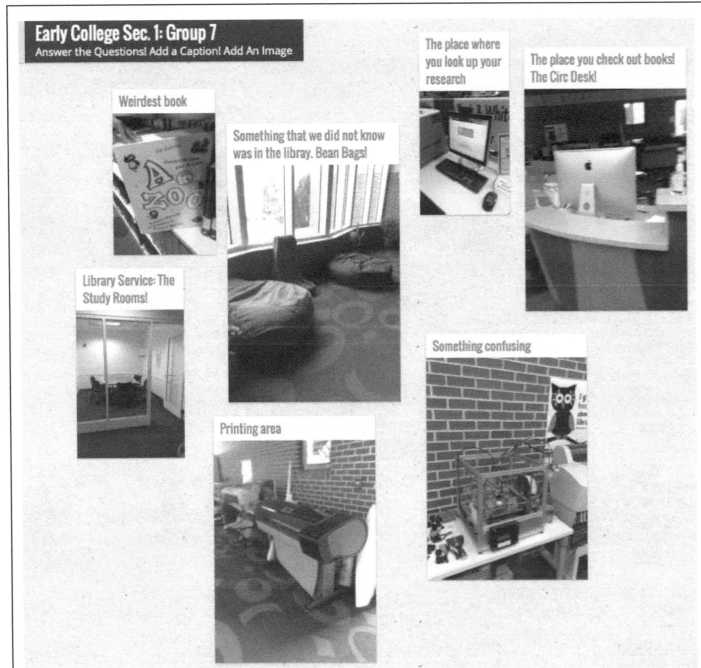

Early College Sec. 1: Group 7
Answer the Questions! Add a Caption! Add An Image

Weirdest book

Something that we did not know was in the libray. Bean Bags!

Library Service: The Study Rooms!

Printing area

The place where you look up your research

The place you check out books! The Circ Desk!

Something confusing

Informed Leadership Fusion

Elizabeth Ponder, Manager of Instruction & Information Services, East Texas Baptist University, eponder@etbu.edu; Emily Row Prevost, Assistant Provost & Assistant Professor of Leadership & Religion, East Texas Baptist University, eprevost@etbu.edu

NUTRITION INFORMATION

This recipe is used as part of a first-year experience curriculum focused on leadership development of students. This fusion recipe asks students to utilize skills in information evaluation to help them build and maintain credibility as a necessary component of leadership. Students learn the value of solid research in making wise decisions, the importance of correct information when communicating as a leader, and the necessity of each of these in building credibility as a leader.

COOKING TIME

- One 50-minute class session
- Students will also be required to come to the library to have an individual consultation with a librarian as homework.

DIETARY GUIDELINES

The goal of this recipe is to enable students to think critically about all information that they consume, create, and share. This lesson helps the students develop an understanding of information authority being constructed and contextual, not only in their academic lives, but also in their personal and professional exchanges. By tying information evaluation to the concepts of credibility in leadership, students are given the tools to think critically about any information that they encounter.

MAIN INGREDIENTS

- ☐ Pre- and post-test for information evaluation
- ☐ 6–8 pre-selected sources on the same topic at varying levels of credibility for in-class evaluation (1 source per student pair, multiple copies of each source can be used)

PREPARATION

- ☐ Begin by selecting an appropriate method for information evaluation. Locate five to six sources on the same topic to allow students to practice the method. Sources should be found at both ends of the credibility spectrum to illustrate the differences in quality of information.
- ☐ The librarian meets with the First-Year Experience Director to identify potential topics for students to research based on collection coverage and appropriateness for beginning researchers.
- ☐ The librarian works with the FYE director to create a pre- and post-test that will assess student ability to evaluate information. Questions are designed to assess both academic and real-world leadership situations in which students would need to evaluate information in the decision-making process.

MAIN COOKING TECHNIQUE

1. Students are given the pre-test at the beginning of class, prior to any instruction on evaluating information. As a part of the leadership curriculum on credibility, students are asked to talk about what happens when we accept bad advice as a leader or get our information from sources that are not very reliable or trustworthy. Instruction should be focused on helping students understand the concept of information evaluation used in all aspects of life.
2. Students receive instruction on the method for information evaluation. Students are then divided into pairs and asked to evaluate a preselected article by applying the model.
3. Once students have evaluated their sources in pairs, ask the class to discuss each source together in order to provide an opportunity to compare and contrast levels of credibility. Option: Use a whiteboard or wall to have students compare their sources by ranking them in relation to one another on a scale of "not credible" to "highly credible."
4. Students are required to select a problem or issue in their community from a predetermined list of possible topics. They will research this issue in order to develop a method for leading change in that area.

5. Students are asked to find at least three sources that they have evaluated as credible and submit them as an annotated bibliography.

6. After meeting individually with a librarian and researching their topic, students are asked to take the post-test to assess their understanding of information evaluation. Instructors use a rubric to evaluate the quality of sources used in the student bibliographies.

ALLERGY WARNINGS

Because instructors often teach FYE classes from various backgrounds, not all FYE instructors feel confident in their ability to teach this information literacy concept. Our solution was to create a brief video tutorial of the information evaluation model to better equip our teachers to provide consistent instruction throughout the program.

CHEF'S NOTE

Students often fail to see the value of information evaluation as a life skill. Though the recipe calls for pre- and post-test questions that emphasize the use of information evaluation as a skill for leadership decision-making and communication, this fusion recipe could be used within any discipline to help students find application for the skills of information evaluation.

This recipe is used in our first-year seminar as one item in a balanced meal of embedded information literacy instruction. Combined with one-on-one visits to meet with a librarian, it has been particularly helpful in introducing the concepts of information evaluation within a broader set of information literacy skills taught in our first-year seminar.

Rolling Through the Library

Judy Geczi, Business Librarian, St. Louis university, jgeczi@att.net

NUTRITION INFORMATION

Webster University Library strives to provide a welcoming environment for its diverse community of students. This recipe spotlights a project that is a collaboration between the library and Webster University's Accessibility Committee. Each year, freshman students are solicited to participate in the library's "Annual Roll Through."

This project provides an opportunity for freshman students to enhance and improve accessibility in the library. Students are placed on teams of at least 4 or 5 people. The roll-through teams navigate the library and the outside surrounding areas with one student operating independently in a wheelchair. The students observe and note potential problems or obstacles for students with physical disabilities and other disabilities, such as visual or hearing impairments, as they navigate the areas. The obstacles might be related to the physical environment in and around the library or to the services the library provides for students in the building.

Examples of items that students reported in the past include, "the restroom door is too heavy to open" and "the wheelchair fits in the group study room, but there was not enough room to turn around." Whether students are part of a roll-through team or just happen to be in the library and are observant on the day of the roll through, they are educated about the daily challenges of students with disabilities.

COOKING TIME

1–3 hours, depending on the size of the library and the number of groups participating.

DIETARY GUIDELINES

The event offers a chance for freshman to experience firsthand the challenges confronting people with disabilities in daily campus life, while at the same time helps the library improve service and accessibility for students with disabilities. This project is an outreach activity that gets students interested in the library and brings student participants to different floors and areas of the library that they might not have otherwise known about or visited. The activity identifies accessibility-related issues in the library that can be investigated further while creating an awareness of what the library offers all students.

MAIN INGREDIENTS

☐ One or more wheelchairs, depending on the size of the library
☐ Clipboards
☐ Accessibility Checklist (Figure 1)

PREPARATION

Customize the Accessibility Checklist to use in your library.

MAIN COOKING TECHNIQUE

1. Divide students into teams.
2. Provide teams with a wheelchair, clipboard, and Accessibility Checklist.
3. Encourage all students to take a turn in the wheelchair.
4. Explain that it is important that as teams go in and out of each room, the person in the wheelchair must access all areas without assistance. (Areas would include group study rooms, restrooms, offices, cafes, elevators, public computer service areas, stacks, etc., as well as the campus areas that immediately surround the library.)
5. Teams note any observed problems or obstacles directly on the Accessibility Checklist.
6. Teams report back to the librarian at a designated place when finished.
7. If multiple teams were formed, the librarian compiles the results into one document.
8. Report fixable items to appropriate staff to resolve issues and/or fix items yourself.

ALLERGY WARNINGS

- Remind students that they should not assist the person in the wheelchair unless absolutely necessary. The teams are trying to mimic real life as much as possible when navigating the library and its surroundings.
- Ask students to provide as much detail as possible when describing a problem. Go over the completed Accessibility Checklist with the team before they depart to clarify the problems they identified.

CHEF'S NOTE

We receive great feedback from our students on changes to make in and around the library. The students help the library create a more inclusive environment and walk-away with possibly a new understanding of how students with disabilities of all types manage in their daily life.

Figure 1 is the Accessibility Checklist adapted from the checklist created by Webster University's Accessibility Committee. The checklist should be customized as appropriate to your library and library space.

FIGURE 1. ACCESSIBILITY CHECKLIST

1. Accessible entrances (easy to get over threshold and open door)
2. Barrier-free access to offices, classrooms, and group study rooms
3. Wheelchair turning space within rooms
4. Accessibility of furniture (table heights, space for wheelchair)
5. Restrooms (barrier-free entrance, easy-open doors, wheelchair turning space, grab bars within stalls)
6. Signage: permanent and daily informational (signage is correct, accessible entrances are identified, permanent signs in Braille)
7. Ease of use of ramps/elevators
8. Navigation of walkways around building
9. Other

A Steaming Bowl of Stone Soup:
Offering a Feast on a Budget

Sarah Copeland, Librarian, Collection Management Librarian, Berry College, scopeland@berry.edu; Becca Decker, Librarian for Information Literacy/Learning Services, Cleveland State Community College, rdecker01@clevelandstatecc.edu

NUTRITION INFORMATION

A community college library creates a fun, academic event that is tailored to support components of a First-Year Seminar (FYS). On a small campus where departments are already stretched thin, the library is a broth to which diverse campus units chip in portions of existing services to cook up a special offering for students. This student-centered event creates big engagement at a low cost.

COOKING TIME

4–6 weeks preparation for the first iteration; 5+ hours active cooking time

DIETARY GUIDELINES

This event serves up opportunities for library outreach and partnerships with other campus departments. Packaged as a fun, late-night event for students, it promotes student success and retention by offering one-stop support for completing a First-Year Seminar course project. It also boosts a sense of community at a commuter college and promotes the library as a place that students want to be.

MAIN INGREDIENTS

- ☐ Extended library hours (11:00 p.m. or midnight for commuter college; later for residential college)
- ☐ Partnership with First-Year Seminar (FYS) with a course-long project
- ☐ Academic support partnerships (e.g., the Writing Center and Instructional Technology) that support FYS course project
- ☐ Healthy snack options, coffee
- ☐ Fun, stress-relieving activities
- ☐ Mix of quiet and group study options; separate space for boisterous activities
- ☐ Optional: Partnership with other campus departments such as Math Lab, Student Activities—the sky's the limit!

PREPARATION

- ☐ Handouts to encourage goal setting and healthy choices
- ☐ Advertising campaign
- ☐ Assessment tools (e.g., post-event surveys)

MAIN COOKING TECHNIQUE

1. Ask the campus community to contribute ingredients (beginning of semester).
   a. Review the FYS curriculum for information about impact of wellness and study behaviors on student success. Sift and set aside for incorporation in Step 3.
   b. Reach out to the FYS Committee to obtain faculty and campus buy-in.

   You may enjoy greater participation at the feast if you season with a dash of extra credit.
   c. In conjunction with the FYS Committee, identify a date and time for the event about 1 week before the course project is due.
   d. Invite academic support, such as the Writing Center and Instructional Technology, to bring ingredients for the Stone Soup. Other campus departments, such as Student Activities or the Math Lab, may also have creative contributions for soup ingredients. Discuss the impact of the event with custodial and security staff.
2. Invite attendees (4 weeks before event).
   a. Determine branding for the event.
   b. Season the event with free promotion strategies, such as campus emails, in-class announcements, announcements to student organizations, social media, promotional tables, and displays. Avoid over-salting with e-mail.
   c. Liberally pepper the campus with posters, table tents, buttons, and other promotional materials made in-house.

3. Combine and bring to a boil (1–2 weeks before event). Throughout this step, incorporate information about wellness and positive study behaviors from the FYS curriculum.
   a. Food and drink. Purchase healthy snacks (e.g., fruit, yogurt) and coffee. Make labels explaining why these are good or comparatively better (e.g., coffee vs. energy drinks) choices when studying.
   b. Academic support partnerships. Confirm participation of academic support personnel. Create placards advertising the type of help each expert will offer at the Panel of Experts. Include reference librarians among the experts.
   c. Create a schedule to promote the designated times for food, activities, and the availability of experts.
   d. Create maps to orient students to quiet areas, activities, location of food, etc. Remember that for many students this will be their first visit to the library!
4. Simmer (day of the event).
   a. Designate a sign-in table in a highly visible location to collect names and emails of attendees. Sign-in facilitates extra credit and assessment.
   b. Designate an area in a high-traffic location for the Panel of Experts.
5. Enjoy a feast of Stone Soup!
   a. When students sign-in, provide them with a schedule of activities, goal-setting handouts, and infor-

mation about where activities are located.
   b. Make unobtrusive announcements about food and activities throughout the event.
   c. Assign library staff to regular circuits of the building to monitor noise levels and assist students.
6. Gather reviews.
   a. Distribute assessment tool(s) to attendees and volunteers.
   b. Analyze results and consider changes to recipe to accommodate local tastes.
   c. Whet everyone's appetite for future events by sharing results of the Stone Soup Feast.

ALLERGY WARNINGS
This event can get loud; be mindful that many commuters are seeking a quiet, focused environment.

CHEF'S NOTE
Stone Soup can be prepared to support any first-year course. Consider availability of local ingredients and adapt the recipe as needed. Stone Soup isn't about the specific ingredients, it is about the community contributions!

Chavez Ravine:
Reshaping the City of Los Angeles

Veronica Ciocia, Reference Librarian, Chapman University, daquino@chapman.edu; Thomas Philo, Archivist/Cataloger, California State University, Dominguez Hills, tphilo@csudh.edu

NUTRITION INFORMATION

Student interactions with primary sources and/or special collections at California State University Dominguez Hills (CSUDH) come mostly in upper-division courses requiring the use of archival materials in their curricula, such as History, English, and Anthropology. Students in these classes are likely to receive instructional sessions led by the Archives Department, and these sessions may constitute the full extent of training many students receive.

Within the scope of the CSUDH Outreach and Information Literacy Program, we aim to provide early exposure to source materials via a co-teaching partnership model for local high school students and college freshmen. This recipe was originally designed to foster students' understanding of the scope and role primary source materials play in scholarship, their relationship to secondary sources and, more important, habits of critical thought.

COOKING TIME

Serves a full room of 35 high school students within the scope of their 90-minute class, but can be adapted to a 75-minute schedule as well. If schedules permit, you will find this recipe exceptionally satisfying and nutritious when provided as a two-shot session.

DIETARY GUIDELINES

- A balanced information literacy diet requires a healthy blend of primary and secondary source research. By addressing this deficiency at the earliest possible time, we hope to help students develop a stronger sense of historical inquiry. These dietary guidelines mix evenly into the larger framework of two threshold concepts: the need to engage with the past in their own terms, and contextualize and interrogate historical sources (Sendziuk 2012).
- The goal of this learning experience is to facilitate a cognitive shift by helping students move away from mere consumers of facts, who only absorb and reproduce knowledge, toward critical thinkers, who understand the nature of historical inquiry and interpretation (Sipress and Voelker 2009).
- Ultimately, a healthy outcome for students who follow these dietary guidelines means they will be able to critically articulate ideas, convey meaning, support arguments in discussion with their peers, and develop a search strategy appropriate to their inquiries and in alignment with the set of primary sources.

MAIN INGREDIENTS

☐ Select primary sources related to local history events with current implications. The construction of Dodger Stadium in Chavez Ravine is considered relevant to the city of Carson's history, not only because our campus was a proposed site for the original stadium, but also in light of its proximity to the recent negotiations related to the construction of the new Los Angeles-based NFL stadium location.

☐ Select information sources providing brief contextual information on the topic. Design prompts for the group discussion activity sheet.

PREPARATION

Prepare seven sets of the following documents: two photographs depicting the events of Chavez Ravine, a reader's letter, a 1959 Los Angeles area map, and an album of photographs depicting the pre-CSUDH grounds. Design a group discussion activity sheet (as a web-based form or print handout) providing contextual information to the topic and set of five questions.

MAIN COOKING TECHNIQUE

Class review and discussion of the definition and types of primary sources, hands-on activity, group discussion, and report of findings

1. Introduction—5 minutes. Librarian provides a brief introduction to the session outline and states clear goals.
2. Class discussion—15 minutes. Librarian and archivist lead class discussion reviewing the definition of primary sources and types, and introduce the Chavez Ravine topic.
3. Document analysis—45 minutes. Seven groups of five students work on document source analysis, using the group discussion web-based activity sheet. Either one student serves as the scribe or each student records one question. The activity includes the following questions:
   a. Compare the two photographs. Describe the people in each photograph. Discuss the idea of power, how it is perceived, and how you would determine who has it. What emotions, if any, do the pictures trigger in you?
   b. Read the letter to the editor. The writer sees a benefit to having a baseball stadium beyond simply a place to play baseball. Is her argument valid? Discuss other arguments (financial, social, cultural). Do such benefits outweigh individual rights against the public benefit?
   c. Look at the Dominguez Estate proposal for Dodger stadium in the South Bay area. Discuss the possible ramifications for having Dodger stadium rather than CSUDH and your school on the current site. What would some of the benefits have been if Dodger stadium was built here? Consider other larger projects, such as freeways. Think where they were developed and who was most affected by their construction. What else has changed since 1959?
   d. How would you go about researching additional information related to the history of Dodger Stadium and Chavez Ravine? Perform a search using the library resources and report two types of information sources you find.
4. Librarian and archivist float the instructional lab and discuss the students' progress. The History teacher calls on each group to discuss the photographs depicting the pre-CSUDH grounds.
5. Report of findings—20 minutes. Ask students to share their responses to the worksheet questions, and ask volunteers to share both their online searching process and the information sources retrieved.
6. Wrap up—5 minutes. Questions, insights, and recap of core concepts.

ALLERGY WARNINGS

- Some students may have difficulties interpreting the context of the photos, even if captions are provided.
- Some students may find it difficult picturing our campus 57 years ago.
- Some students may find it challenging analyzing the space when viewing the map—for example, finding patterns and thinking in terms of the cultural effects of distance.

CHEF'S NOTE

The selections of primary sources and prompts could be easily adjusted to suit different educational levels and academic needs. The lesson may be seasoned according to taste with links to online photographs, clippings, reports, and other primary materials available in libraries and archives, to give students a flavor of the resources available. Students are more engaged when the topic is connected to their personal history and are more motivated when they realize how these skills can transfer to their own research projects.

SET OF PRIMARY SOURCES USED:

- Deighton, Valda K. "Invaluable Contributions." *Los Angeles Times*, January 23, 1959, Proquest Historical Newspapers (167405743).
- Map, Proposed Location for L.A. Dodgers' Ballpark, January, 1958. Rancho San Pedro Collection, Box 264, Folder 3599. California State University Archives & Special Collections.
- Walker, Bill. "Formal Pact Signed for Dodgers' New Home." June 4, 1959. *Herald Examiner* Collection Photographs, Los Angeles Public Library

Images. Accessed, June 13, 2016 http://jpg2.lapl.org/pics42/00055805.jpg
- "Eviction in Chavez Ravine" May 11, 1959. *Herald Examiner* Collection Photographs, Los Angeles Public Library Images. Accessed, June 13, 2016 http://jpg2.lapl.org/pics32/00050963.jpg

REFERENCES FOR DIETARY GUIDELINES

- Sendziuk, Paul. "Helping Students to Think Historically by Engaging Threshold Concepts." In *Threshold Concepts: From Personal Practice to Communities of Practice, Proceedings of the National Academy's Sixth Annual Conference*, Dublin, Ireland, 28–29 June 2012.
- Sipress, Joel M. and David J. Voelker. 2009. "From Learning History to Doing History: Beyond the Coverage Model." Chap. 2 in *Exploring Signature Pedagogies* edited by Regan A.R. Gurung, Nancy L. Chick, and Aeron Haynie. Sterling: Stylus.

May I Take Your Order?
Student Library Advisory Group
Beth Daniel Lindsay, Access and Public Services Librarian, NYU Abu Dhabi beth.lindsay@nyu.edu

NUTRITION INFORMATION

A student library advisory group serves as a conduit for information, requests, and feedback between the wider student body and the library. The members of the advisory group gain insight into the workings of the library and can offer suggestions for and evaluations of library services. They provide an easy-to-access group for qualitative feedback.

For example, we recently conducted a LibQual survey. Once we had the survey results, we presented the results to library staff and the advisory group. In turn, the advisory group made suggestions and commented on our ideas for changes to implement based on the survey. They also theorized with us as to what might have prompted some of the more confusing comments.

COOKING TIME

3 one-hour meetings per semester (once per month minus the last month)

DIETARY GUIDELINES

- A student library advisory group can help any library that is interested in learning more about its students formalize the feedback process to improve the student experience.

- In addition to providing the library with a valuable assessment tool, the student advisory group can also help with library outreach.

MAIN COOKING TECHNIQUE

Focus group

MAIN INGREDIENTS

- ☐ 1–2 motivated librarians
- ☐ 4–10 students

PREPARATION

1–3 hours preparation and follow-up time per meeting, depending on suggestions received

MAIN COOKING METHOD

1. Identify a group of students who are motivated to provide feedback about the library. We work with student government and have found that most volunteers are first-year students. However, others may find it useful to reach out to other student groups, such as a student book club. Library student employees are another possibility. A blended or parallel approach may also be appropriate, whereby meetings are held with multiple groups independently based on their affiliation or availability.

2. Select meeting times. We request course schedules for the student members and suggest times accordingly via a Doodle poll. We particularly aim for lunch meetings, so we can provide food as additional incentive/thank you.

3. Set an agenda. The first meeting is usually a get-to-know-you affair. Set the parameters for the group—this is an advisory group, not a dictatorship. Subsequent meetings can address more detailed issues. Select one to two questions/issues per meeting to allow for plenty of discussion time and so that students can bring their own issues.

4. Meet. During the meeting, focus on listening to what the students have to say. Take notes, if they do not.

5. Review the notes with student advisory group members and share with your library team.

6. Identify action items and work toward accomplishing those in tandem with the advisory group when appropriate and possible.

7. Close the loop! Update the advisory group with any actions you have taken/ changes you have made based on their feedback. If you choose not to implement suggestions, explain why. Don't be defensive or rest on reasons like "we've always done it this way."

8. Shout it from the rooftops. Promote the changes/initiatives directly to the student body and reference the origins in the advisory group. This reinforces the importance of the group, can recruit future members, and lead to more suggestions to/from the group.

ALLERGY WARNINGS

Ensure that students understand that you may not be able to implement all their ideas, but are open to hearing them. This is an advisory group, not a policy-making board.

CHEF'S NOTE

- Success can be dependent on selection of student members of the group.
- The suggestions we've received from our student advisory group vary widely from prohibiting food in the silent study room to restocking markers in the group study rooms. The student advisory group can also be a source for structured user experience testing, since the group is already formed. The group can also help recruit other students for user experience testing and/ or other focus groups.
- The student advisory group also helps us with promoting our posts on social media. Facebook is by far the most popular platform on our campus, and they routinely "like" our posts. We also ask them to share select posts on a private, students-only page.
- Our student advisory group was a strong advocate for the creation of a leisure reading collection. Now that we have created the collection, we continue to accept suggestions from all students, but particularly from the advisory group.

Collaboration with Undergraduate Research Office to Create "Join the Research Conversation" Workshop

Elizabeth L. Black, Associate Professor and Undergraduate Engagement Librarian, Ohio State University Libraries, black.367@osu.edu

NUTRITION INFORMATION

The Join the Research Conversation workshop introduces students to undergraduate research and supports them in the difficult task of identifying potential faculty research mentors on campus through the context of Scholarship as a Conversation. It is one offering of a multifaceted collaborative partnership with the Undergraduate Research Office that includes: other workshops; library hosting the fall research forum and winning posters from the larger spring undergraduate research forum; and peer mentors staffing a table in the library near the reference desk for 10 hours a week for most weeks of the semester to help students get started in research.

COOKING TIME

Workshop duration is 75 minutes.

DIETARY GUIDELINES

Both librarians and offices of undergraduate research support research, yet collaborations between the two groups do not come naturally. One challenge is the word "research" and its meaning in the two different contexts. In a library, research generally means searching, selecting, and using literature. In an undergraduate research context, research is "an inquiry or investigation conducted by an undergraduate student that makes an original intellectual or creative contribution to the discipline." (Council on Undergraduate Research, n.d.) The literature, or library, research is only a small part of this research.

ACRL FRAMEWORK ADDRESSED

The Framework for Information Literacy and specifically the concept of Scholarship as a Conversation provide a useful metaphor for connecting information literacy, including and beyond traditional library instruction, to the undergraduate research experience.

MAIN INGREDIENTS

☐ Classroom or meeting room (can be held in residence hall lounge)
☐ Ask students to bring their own devices
☐ iPads or laptops for those who don't have own a device
☐ Undergraduate Research Office (URO) staff member
☐ Handouts from URO
☐ Worksheet for hands-on portion

PREPARATION

Connect with your local Undergraduate Research Office or equivalent. This workshop is most effective when both the library and that office are full participants.

MAIN COOKING TECHNIQUE

1. Begin session with an upper-class student involved in Undergraduate Research sharing their experiences, focusing on why it has been valuable to them and how they got started.
2. Librarian provides a short presentation explaining how research is like a conversation by asking students to recall different types of conversations they have had, including in-person and written conversations. Ask students if conversations can happen over time.
3. Explain that they can look through publications in the academic literature. Pass out screen-shots of citation maps from Web of Science. Ask students what they represent.
4. Guided by a worksheet, students brainstorm keywords that describe their interest. Using their own device or one provided by the library, students use Scopus or Web of Science to identify individuals at their institution who have published research in areas of their interest.
5. As students are working, the librarian and the URO staff member are checking in with the students, answering questions, and providing tips. It is often during this time that powerful, personalize instruction happens.

6. Students identify a next action for themselves to get involved in undergraduate research.

CHEF'S NOTE
Other approaches to working with Undergraduate Research offices through the lens of the frame Scholarship as Conversation were discussed in *Neighbors Helping Neighbors: Partnering with Undergraduate Research Offices to Present Scholarship as a Conversation* at the LOEX conference on May 6, 2016. The presentation is posted at http://www.loexconference.org/presentations/LOEX2016_Neighbors%20Helping%20Neighbors.pdf.

WORKS CITED
Council on Undergraduate Research. (n.d.) Frequently Asked Questions. Retrieved from http://www.cur.org/about_cur/frequently_asked_questions_/#2.

PART IV. ASSESSMENT

Instructional and First Year Experience Assessment

How Was Your Meal?
Post-instruction Assessment of FY Classes

Donna E. Coghill, Community Engagement Librarian, VCU Libraries, decoghil@vcu.edu; Jennifer A. Stout, Teaching & Learning Librarian, VCU Libraries, jastout@vcu.edu; Rachel A. McCaskill, Learning Technologies Librarian, VCU Libraries, ramccaskill@vcu.edu

NUTRITION INFORMATION

Virginia Commonwealth University (VCU) Libraries cooks up various library instruction sessions for core classes, including UNIV 112 and UNIV 200. UNIV 112 is a first-year, 3-credit, writing-intensive course that incorporates elements of VCU's Core Curriculum, including critical thinking and information literacy. Each library instruction session includes one librarian, one faculty member, one classroom, and approximately 20 students.

Following each prepared meal (library instruction session), chefs (librarians) use a Google Form to track the dietary and nutritional elements of each meal. A 5-point Likert scale is used to track the extent the class focused on each learning outcome. For example, a librarian may assign a "4" to "Search Term Development" and a "1" to "Google Scholar" to indicate that much of the class focused on learning how to develop keywords and search terms, while Google Scholar was only briefly shown.

Chefs fill out their own post-meal card (Google Form) to rate the dining (classroom) experience. The form not only includes the quantitative meal (instruction) assessment, but also a blank box at the end of the

form for qualitative assessment. This box captured information including additional nutritional components of the meal, such as learning outcomes or research tools not listed in the quantitative form above.

COOKING TIME

- Library classes are either 50 minutes or 75 minutes
- Preparation time varies by librarian
- Time it takes to fill out the Google form is about 5 minutes
- Data analysis, ongoing

DIETARY GUIDELINES

This post-dining assessment was created to help VCU Libraries determine whether we as chefs are serving what we think we are serving, whether our patrons' palates are appreciating the nuanced flavors in their meals, and whether we are meal prepping in the most effective way to achieve the goal of creating more sophisticated palates among our patrons.

The goal of this assessment is to see patterns in what librarians cover (and, tacitly, what course instructors request that we cover) across all UNIV 112 and 200 library sessions. Despite the "spiral curriculum" in UNIV 112 and 200 (meaning instructors in

200 circle back to some concepts covered in 112, including information literacy learning outcomes), librarians aim to distinguish content taught in 112 and 200 so that students who attend a library session for both courses do not feel as though they are getting the exact same dining experience twice. The projected longer-term goal is to map what we cover in these meals to the ACRL Framework.

MAIN INGREDIENTS

☐ Sous-chef (faculty) with research assignment

☐ Patrons (students) in a classroom environment

☐ Chef (librarian) with lesson plan and learning outcomes

☐ Post-meal Card (assessment form): Access to Google Forms, or a similar form/survey creation platform, is required. Template form: http://tinyurl.com/postinstructreport

PREPARATION

Create an online assessment form in Google Forms.

MAIN COOKING TECHNIQUE

Assessment form via Google Forms

COOKING METHOD

To create the assessment form: work together with your instruction team to create a menu of the most common concepts taught in your FYE library instruction classes. These could include "Keyword development," "Evaluating resources," "Database searching," etc. They may also be unique to your institution or information literacy program. Each meal is different!

Using Google Forms, or a similar platform, create an assessment form listing each concept with the option to select 1 through 5 (1 being "didn't cover at all" and 5 being "spent most of the class on this"). Additionally, it is recommended to have a blank box at the end of the form, where librarians can record notes or additional concepts covered. The most important aspect of this meal evaluation (assessment) is the precise tracking of patterns.

The next important part of the preparation process is the collaboration with the sous-chef, the course instructor. Librarians and course instructors work together and pull from the menu of options to create a delicious meal for students that addresses the specific dietary needs of that class. Here is a partial menu of what Virginia Commonwealth University librarians and course instructors whipped up:

- Refining/developing research questions
- Developing search terms
- Using the VCU Libraries Search to find books and articles
- Evaluating resources
- Learning how to contact librarians for additional help

ALLERGY WARNINGS

May include sous-chefs who are less hands-on than anticipated during the meal prep phase.

CHEF'S NOTE

After a semester of recording what we covered in 34 UNIV 112 classes, we saw that the major areas of focus in UNIV 112 were: developing search terms/strategy; finding resources in our discovery tool, VCU Libraries Search; refining research questions; and differentiating types of sources. UNIV 112 library sessions tend to be a more basic meal than UNIV 200—more chicken fingers and french fries, as opposed to the pecan-crusted chicken with lemon-herb reduction and roasted red potatoes in UNIV 200 library sessions. In UNIV 112, students are introduced to library tools and research skills on a basic level, enough to get them through their assignments in class. In UNIV 200, librarians introduce new, more complex flavors.

While focusing our first meal (library instruction session) on the information literacy needs of the first-year student in UNIV 112, and our second meal on the more advanced abilities of the UNIV 200 student, our ultimate goal is to build a more mature information literacy palate for the upper-level undergraduate dietary needs.

Infographic Pie Judging in a Science FYS

Sarah Oelker, Science Librarian, Mount Holyoke College, soelker@mtholyoke.edu; Katherine Aidala, Associate Professor of Physics, Mount Holyoke College, kaidala@mtholyoke.edu

NUTRITION INFORMATION
This exercise is intended for a First-Year Seminar (FYS) on media coverage of science and/or issues such as race or gender in STEM. The assessment questions, however, are general enough to be used across many FYS library sessions; sharing is caring!

NUMBERS SERVED
10–20

COOKING TIME
40 minutes

DIETARY GUIDELINES
Critique an infographic in small groups and find related scholarship, with pre- and post-class qualitative assessment.

ACRL FRAMEWORKS ADDRESSED
- Authority Is Constructed and Contextual
- Information Creation as a Process

MAIN INGREDIENTS
- ☐ Computer lab, laptop cart, or students equipped with their own laptops
- ☐ Internet access
- ☐ Online survey tool or learning management system for administering the pre- and post-assessments

- An infographic suitable for the exercise, which gives leads to scholarly studies. We used http://benschmidt.org/profGender for this exercise. Familiarize yourself with the leads to scholarly studies before doing the exercise.
- Worksheet or slides with the discussion prompts (optional)

MAIN COOKING TECHNIQUE
Pre-assessment, hands-on exercise, small group work, post-assessment

PREPARATION
Before the session, ask students to find a brief article on a scientific finding, and turn in their article along with a single-page reading response. Provide a library guide with a listing of media sources on science (newspapers, blogs, podcasts, etc.). After this assignment is due, but *before* students meet with the librarian, ask the following pre-assessment questions as an assignment or survey:
1. What's been easy to find so far?
2. What have you had trouble finding?
3. What questions do you have for the librarian about finding appropriate resources for this class?

COOKING METHOD
1. Begin class by showing an anonymous summary of student responses, and discuss them.
2. Have students form groups of two or three. Introduce students to an infographic. Ask students to investigate this web page and graphic together (but no other sources), and discuss these questions:
   » What is this infographic saying?
   » How strong of a case does it make?
   » After 3–5 minutes, ask groups to share their answers.
3. Ask students to search the web for more information, using links on the infographic page or by any other search method desired. Ask them to consider these questions:
   » Where did the data come from?
   » How was this made, and do you agree with their choices?
   » Who made this? What is their training? Are they associated with any interest groups?
   » After 3–5 minutes, ask groups to share what they found.
4. Next, choose a study that is related to the infographic and, as a group, navigate to the full text of the article. Have the groups discuss it, asking the questions:

» Is it related?
» Is it scholarly?
» Is it peer reviewed?
» How can you tell?
» After 3–5 minutes, ask groups to share their findings.

5. A few days after the library session, have students answer these questions in an assignment or survey:
   » What did you learn that was new to you in our session in the library?
   » What did we cover in the library session that you already knew? You don't have to give an exhaustive list, just a few examples of the first few things that come to mind.
   » What questions about finding information have arisen for you since our library session?

ALLERGY WARNINGS
- If possible, give participation or homework credit for the pre- and post-assessments.
- Make clear that the points are for responding, not for specific responses.
- Make clear that anonymous student responses to the pre-assessment will be shown in class.

CHEF'S NOTE
Consider discussing these questions after completing this recipe:
- Scientific studies have complex language. Where can you look up unfamiliar words?

- Scientific studies are dense. Do you have to read them in order? Would reading out of order help your comprehension? Invite the course instructor to talk about the order in which they read studies.

Whetting the Intellect with Sources:
Considering the Continuum of Information Sources

Jennie E. Callas, Coordinator of Reference and Instruction, University of Wisconsin-Parkside Library, callas@uwp.edu

NUTRITION INFORMATION

First-year students often evaluate and characterize information sources simplistically. They may believe dot-com websites are always unreliable and books make the best sources. But college-level research requires more nuance. This activity uses a worksheet to facilitate discussion of the variety of information sources and their suitability for assorted information needs.

COOKING TIME

30–50 minutes

DIETARY GUIDELINES

This activity helps students understand how a wide range of information sources can meet the needs of both formal and informal research.

ACRL FRAMEWORKS ADDRESSED

- Information Creation as a Process
- Authority is Constructed and Contextual

MAIN COOKING TECHNIQUE

Worksheet and group discussion

MAIN INGREDIENTS

- ☐ One worksheet for each student
- ☐ A computer with projector

PREPARATION

- ☐ Optional: Ask the instructor to assign students to watch a video on the Information Cycle (see below for one possibility). Watching this ahead of time will whet their intellect for the activity to come.
- ☐ Prepare and print the blank "types of information sources" worksheet (see http://tinyurl.com/cookbookinfosource), so each student has one.
- ☐ Prepare the comprehensive version, which has one additional column, to fill out as a group during the discussion (see http://tinyurl.com/cookbookinfosourcecomp).
- ☐ Depending on the needs of the research assignment (if there is one), you may want to pre-populate the first column of the comprehensive worksheet with information sources you absolutely want to cover, leaving room to add others depending on how much time you have.

MAIN COOKING METHOD

1. Tell students that they will be working as a group to describe different kinds of information sources and to recognize research situations in which those sources will be useful. Give one blank worksheet to each student, and ask them to complete as much of it as they can in five minutes.

2. After five minutes, ask students to pair up (or form small groups) and compare their charts for another 2–3 minutes. This will prompt them to add even more items or details.

3. Project the comprehensive worksheet and point out the additional fourth column, which you will be working on as a group. Complete the chart, with the librarian typing and asking follow-up questions while it's projected. If you prepopulated the first column, start with those items.

4. After the session, clean up the document so the instructor can include it in her course site. It can be a resource for students with a research assignment as they consider the information sources they should look for.

ALLERGY WARNINGS

- If students are reluctant to participate, go around the room, so each student, pair, or small group completes one row. The rest of the class can contribute if they also identified that type of source.
- Students may be too vague, e.g. naming "the internet" as a type of source. Ask them to be more specific. They may also get stuck in the rut of tra-

ditional print sources. Probe them to identify media, such as online videos, podcasts, tweets, etc. Ask them to consider situations, such as researching a popular music group, current event, or an issue affecting the college/university.

- Sample comprehensive worksheet for class/group discussion: http://tinyurl.com/cookbookinfosourcecomp.

CHEF'S NOTES

- This activity works without a research assignment. If there is an assignment, use the activity at the start of the research process. Make sure the instructor will allow students to use many kinds of sources in their research.
- With groups of more than 30 students, have small discussion groups complete the comprehensive worksheet. Circulate to guide them.
- Options for adapting this activity to a short timeframe include:
  » Have students begin their brainstorm before class or in pairs for 5 minutes or even less (distribute one worksheet per pair, which will ensure they work together).
  » Prepopulate the student worksheet's first column with the kinds of resources you want to focus on discussing.

ADDITIONAL RESOURCES

- Loftis, E. (Narrator). (2015). Information cycle [Online video]. Retrieved from Lynda.com.
- Sample worksheet for individual work: http://tinyurl.com/cookbookinfosource.

Culinary Fusion:
Integrating Information Literacy into a General Education Menu using the LEAP Toolkit

Laura Baker, Librarian for Digital Research and Learning, Abilene Christian University Library, bakerl@acu.edu

NUTRITION INFORMATION

This recipe uses the recommendations from the Liberal Education and America's Promise (LEAP) toolkit from the Association of American Colleges and Universities (AAC&U) to infuse information literacy into a university general education program. It uses best practices to create an assignment that encourages interdisciplinary thinking and to assess targeted research skills.

At Abilene Christian University, the first course in the freshman core is called Cornerstone. Cornerstone exists to equip students to think and communicate in an interdisciplinary way. It is also the first introduction to college research expectations. Students work on an annotated bibliography throughout the course. At semester's end, an assessment team uses a rubric to evaluate the bibliographies to determine skills learned.

The student assignment represents a degree of integration between library and course goals with very effective results, and the assessment rubric allows the library to document learning success.

COOKING TIME

Ideally, this is a semester-long diet, but it can be modified into a nutrient-dense meal over a few weeks.

DIETARY GUIDELINES

Annotated bibliography

MAIN COOKING TECHNIQUE

Annotated bibliography, LEAP rubric

MAIN INGREDIENTS

- ☐ A collaborative relationship with the department responsible for the freshman general education core
- ☐ A commitment to following through with end-of-semester assessment

PREPARATION

Professor Chefs: Course professors spend class time talking about majors, the differences in academic disciplines, and how these disciplines approach learning.

Librarian Chefs: Create a web page or research guide to collect suggested sources and tutorials that will help students compile their bibliographies. Good choices for the guide are lists of databases by discipline, tutorials for searching a database, criteria for evaluating sources, and examples of proper citation. The guide should be embedded in the course Content Management System or made accessible from the library web page.

MAIN COOKING METHOD

1. Professors introduce the annotated bibliography as a natural follow-up to previous explorations of the different academic disciplines and how they approach learning. A librarian is invited into the class to introduce themselves, to show the research guide and how it can be used, and to offer their availability as Sherpas in the research process.
2. Each student will compile an annotated bibliography using sources from a variety of disciplines (assignment below). In this manner, students explore the same topic from multiple perspectives and learn how different disciplines see the world. In so doing, they learn basic research skills appropriate to college expectations.
3. Instructions are given to students: Cornerstone Annotated Bibliography.
4. Choose a topic that sparks your curiosity and that can be explored through at least two of the different academic disciplines (natural science, social science, humanities, fine arts, theology).
5. Find ten sources important to the understanding of your topic. Sources should meet the following criteria:
   - » Sources must be relevant and appropriate to the research question.

» The list of sources should represent at least two of the academic disciplines (natural science, social science, humanities, fine arts, theology).

» You should have at least four sources from each of two different disciplines. The remaining two sources can be from whatever discipline you choose, either more of your main two disciplines or from the other academic disciplines.

» At least two sources from each discipline should be found physically in the library.

» Strive for a variety of sources (books, journal articles, websites).

6. For each source, include the full citation in MLA style followed by a 200-word annotation. The annotation should consist of two paragraphs.

» First paragraph: Summary of the source's argument and main points

» Second paragraph: Your assessment of the source's validity and usefulness (use the CRAAP test).

The annotated bibliography works well if scaffolded or broken into manageable units:

- Week 1: Choosing a topic
- Week 2: Formulating a research question
- Week 3: Finding sources
- Week 4: Evaluating sources
- Week 5: Writing annotations
- Week 6: Putting the whole paper together

At the end of the semester, an assessment committee composed of faculty from each academic discipline, including the library, collects copies of the annotated bibliographies and selects a sample for evaluation.

Evaluation is based on the Information Literacy VALUE rubric developed by AAC&U. As AAC&U recommended, we translated the language of the basic rubric into the language of our campus's general education program. Our rubric is in Figure 1.

Scores from the sampled assignments are averaged and tracked over time to gauge the degree to which students have mastered a baseline level of research skills.

ALLERGY WARNINGS

Students will need the most help simply in thinking broadly enough about their topics in order to find a variety of sources in more than one discipline. Be prepared to help them brainstorm solutions other than the obvious ones.

CHEF'S NOTE

The assignment: The secret sauce for this recipe is the degree to which the annotated bibliography is infused into the overall goals of the freshman course. The assignment is not a standalone "library assignment" created to give students a reason to use the library. It is an assignment that fulfills the broader goals of the course and of enlarging one's worldview. Such integration avoids the empty-calorie effect of an artificial assignment created just to give students research practice.

In true fusion-cuisine fashion, the assignment draws on elements of different traditions and blends them into a unique experience. The assignment can be adjusted to reflect the mix of disciplines stressed at any campus. Pick the regional cuisines that work for you!

The assessment: Results of student work traditionally have been hard for libraries to obtain for assessment purposes. By tying the assessment to general education outcomes, supported not only by the course but also by the LEAP initiatives, the library is more likely to gain support for and interest in assessing actual student work.

ADDITIONAL RESOURCES

- Association of American Colleges and Universities. "Information Literacy VALUE Rubric." *Association of American Colleges and Universities*. AAC&U. 31 July 2014. Web. 26 May 2016. https://www.AAC&U.org/value/rubrics/information-literacy.
- *LEAP Campus Toolkit*. Association of American Colleges and Universities. n.d. Web. 26 May 2016. http://leap.AAC&U.org/toolkit/.

Rubric Items		Exemplary (4)	Competent (3)	Emerging (2)	Unacceptable (1)	Score
ONE	Determine the nature and the extent of information needed	Effectively defines and narrows the scope of the research question/topic.	Defines the scope of the research question/topic completely.	Defines the scope of the research question/topic or incompletely (parts are missing, remains too broad or too narrow, etc.).	Has difficulty defining the scope of the research question/topic.	
	Obj 1.1.A	Types of information (sources) selected directly relate to concepts or answer research questions.	Types of information (sources) selected relate to concepts or answer research question.	Types of information (sources) selected partially relate to concepts or answer research questions.	Types of information (sources) selected do not relate to concepts or answer research questions.	
TWO	Access the needed information effectively and efficiently	Citations represent various scholarly or academic sources All cited resources come from reliable sources All resources are appropriate for the target audience.	Most citations represent scholarly or academic sources Most cited resources come from reliable sources Most resources are appropriate for the target audience	Citations represent a limited range of scholarly or academic sources Some cited resources come from reliable sources Some resources are appropriate for the target audience	Citations are from only one scholarly or academic source Few cited resources come from reliable sources Few resources are appropriate for the target audience.	
	Obj 1.1.B					
THREE	Access and use information ethically and legally (information use strategies)	Citations and references are correct MLA citation style.	Citations and references are MLA style with few errors.	Citations and references are consistent, but aren't MLA style.	Citations and references do not resemble a citation style.	
	Obj 1.1.C	Paraphrase, summary, or quotes in ways that are true to original context.	Paraphrase, summary, or quotes are close to the original context, but not rely too heavily on quoting or have too little summary.	Paraphrase, summary, or quotes are too broad to reflect the original content.	Annotations are absent or do not reflect content of the article.	

FIGURE 1. ANNOTATED BIBLIOGRAPHY RUBRIC

Practicing Peer Review

Christina Heady, Coordinator of First-Year Instruction and Assistant Professor, Southern Illinois University, cheady@lib.siu.edu;
Joshua Vossler, Head of Reference and Instruction and Associate Professor, Southern Illinois University, jvossler@lib.siu.edu

NUTRITION INFORMATION

Instructors frequently request that we teach their first-year students how to locate peer-reviewed articles in library databases, but their students rarely arrive knowing what a peer-reviewed article is. This knowledge gap needs to be overcome before we can successfully teach students what the instructors want them to know.

This recipe was created to deal with the problem of explaining peer review to first-year students by engaging them in an exercise that mimics aspects of the peer-review process in order to make the explanation of peer-review more meaningful.

COOKING TIME

15-minute icebreaker activity

DIETARY GUIDELINES

This recipe is designed to efficiently introduce students to the concept of peer-review prior to teaching them how to locate peer-reviewed articles in library databases. The purpose is to introduce and explain the peer-review process as useful but flawed, and to avoid positioning peer-reviewed articles as infallible sources of truth.

ACRL FRAMEWORK ADDRESSED

Authority is Constructed and Contextual:

Use research tools and indicators of authority to determine the credibility of sources, understanding the elements that might temper this credibility.

MAIN COOKING TECHNIQUE

This icebreaker is a form of formative assessment. Circulate around the room while students are working in small groups, provide them with constructive feedback, and take note of any trends in how they react to the statements. Spend a few minutes addressing the room at the end of the activity and use what you learned about the students to tweak your lesson plan. For a more skeptical group, for example, emphasize that they should not throw the baby out with the bathwater just because we cannot be sure whether something is 100 percent true or false.

MAIN INGREDIENTS

A collection of 30 true and false statements. If you plan to teach multiple sections using this recipe, we recommend having at least two complete copies of the true and false statements, as some of the statements are likely to go missing or become damaged from session to session.

True statements can range from mundane to amusing:

- The Moon orbits the Earth.
- Hippopotamuses will spin their tales while they defecate in order to create a spray of fecal matter.

False statements can vary from comically implausible to profoundly bizarre:

- The sun, as well as all of the stars, revolve around the Earth.
- The aquatic monkey that lives in your toilet wants you to learn yoga.

PREPARATION

Select 15 facts (or true statements) that can be expressed in one sentence or less (facts about animals seem to work well). Then create 15 utterly false statements. These statements can be tailored to your audience. We enjoy making the false statements especially odd or comical, both for the sense of fun it brings, but also to emphasize that peer review is best able to weed out dramatically bizarre ideas, so the more bizarre the false statements are, the better.

Once both sets of statements are ready, print them out and cut the sheets so each statement is on its own piece of paper. One could also write the statements onto note cards. Shuffle the false and true statements together and you are ready to go.

MAIN COOKING METHOD

1. Divide students into groups of three. (2 minutes)
2. Hand each student one statement. (2 minutes)
3. Give students activity instructions: "Read your statement. If you think it is true, pass it to your left. If you think it is false, place it face-down. Once everyone in the group has read and accepted or rejected each statement, raise your hand and I'll collect them." (1 minute)
4. Give students time to read and accept or reject the statements. Collect the statements as each group finishes, but keep the accepted and rejected piles separate. (5 minutes)
5. Count the statements students decided were true. Share the number with the class.
6. Explain the activity: "What you just did is basically peer review, the process scholarly articles go through before they can be published. Real peer review is much more complicated than right and wrong, and real research is rarely this cut and dried. This exercise shows one of the many advantages of peer review: weeding out research that's obviously crazy. Which you all did a pretty good job at." (5 minutes)
7. Read 1–3 examples of false statements that made it through. Explain that when the really crazy stuff is already gone, what you're left with might not be perfect, but it's pretty good. And that saves time. When you're searching in library databases, you don't have to worry about whether or not an article you found is crazy; peer reviewers already did that for you. They also checked the methodology and other useful things that you might not have the time to do for yourself. That doesn't mean the article is completely true, though. It's just probably not crazy.

ALLERGY WARNINGS

- Students have a tendency to think in binary—everything is either true or false. Before the activity, stress to students that there are *both* kinds of statements in their group. That way they won't claim that none of their statements are true.
- By using true and false statements, however, this exercise inadvertently implies that scholarly research is also either right or wrong. Reality tends to be much more complicated and messy, which is important to emphasize to first-year students.

CHEF'S NOTE

This recipe gives a strong first impression before launching into database searching. Instructors appreciate that this activity emphasizes the nuances of peer review. It paints a more complete picture of the material they are required to use and explains why we ask them to evaluate everything, including scholarly articles.

We All Read the Same Book:
Assessing the Impact of the Common Reader

Jenny Harris, Education and Social Sciences Librarian, Austin Peay State University, harrisj@apsu.edu; Jamie Addy, First-Year Librarian, Georgia College, jame.addy@gcsu.edu

NUTRITION INFORMATION

While Georgia College has implemented a successful Common Reader program for many years, no formalized assessment has occurred. In Fall 2015, during the university's Week of Welcome, which takes places the week prior to the start of classes, all incoming students were encouraged to read *The Other Wes Moore* by Wes Moore.

Russell Library decided to capture assessment data on the Common Reader experience by targeting students with undeclared majors and facilitating reading circles to measure their engagement with the text. This was the first time Russell Library formally participated in the program.

NUMBERS SERVED

200 students (in groups of 20)

COOKING TIME

45 minutes

DIETARY GUIDELINES

This recipe can be used as a model for other Common Reader programs and as an example of how to leverage the library for university-wide outreach and assessment.

ACRL FRAMEWORKS ADDRESSED

- Information Has Value
- Scholarship as Conversation

MAIN COOKING TECHNIQUE

Small group discussion, reflection, and exit ticket assessment

MAIN INGREDIENTS

- ☐ Common Reader text/book/activity
- ☐ Discussion questions/LibGuide
- ☐ Flip charts
- ☐ Exit ticket worksheet

PREPARATION

- ☐ Prior to the Week of Welcome, encourage volunteers from the library to lead small group discussions focused on the Common Reader book.
- ☐ Identify group or individual facilitators and pre-divide all students with undeclared majors among the facilitators.
- ☐ Determine locations throughout the building to host small group discussions.
- ☐ Compile information on the Common Reader book, the author, and other relevant information, such as convocation activities into a resource guide (LibGuide).

- » Feature discussion questions and themes found in the text on the LibGuide.
- ☐ Disseminate the LibGuide to other campus stakeholders as a way to generate student discussion about the text. (A link to our LibGuide can be found here: http://libguides.gcsu.edu/convocation.)

MAIN COOKING METHOD

1. Greet students as they arrive and separate into groups of 20 students (a librarian/library staff member pair works well).
2. Lead students to pre-determined discussion areas equipped with pencils, visual discussion aids (such as whiteboards or paper flip charts), and the exit ticket assessment.
3. Engage students in conversation about the text to encourage critical thinking skills.
4. Five minutes before the allotted time is up, provide students with the exit ticket worksheet to complete. Our ticket asked students the following questions:
   - » How much of *The Other Wes Moore* did you read?
   - » How would you rate this experience?

> » How has reading and discussing *The Other Wes Moore* impacted your personal development?
> » Do you feel this activity is a good introduction to Georgia College? Why or why not?

5. Collect exit tickets as students leave the discussion group.

ALLERGY WARNINGS

Students may not have read the book. This is a pitfall of any Common Reader program that is not fully integrated within the First-Year curriculum. Facilitators should pull out major themes from the book and have a list of questions prepared to guide the conversation.

CHEF'S NOTE

Assessment of this activity was well received by university administration. While the discussion component has been in place for many years, a way to capture meaningful assessment has not previously been implemented. Going forward, the library will assess *all* students participating in the Common Reader program and provide input on how to better integrate the selected text throughout the first-year experience.

Taste Testing for Two:
Using Formative and Summative Assessment

Elisa Slater Acosta, Instruction Coordinator, Loyola Marymount University, elisa.acosta@lmu.edu; Katherine Donaldson, Social Sciences/Education Librarian, University of Oregon, kdonalds@uoregon.edu

NUTRITION INFORMATION

This activity was created to introduce first-year students to library resources they can use for their annotated bibliography assignment. In pairs, students are assigned a task card that requires them to find an information source. After finding a source meeting the criteria of their task card, the student teams input their answers into a Google Form. Formative assessment takes place during class, allowing the librarian to modify instruction on-the-spot based on the responses from the form.

Summative assessment takes place at the end of the semester, when a rubric is applied to a sample of student responses from the activity. This assessment provides a more thorough picture of where students may have succeeded or struggled with the activity, and may provide ideas for how to adjust the activity in the future.

COOKING TIME
20–30 minutes

ACRL FRAMEWORK ADDRESSED
Searching as Strategic Exploration

MAIN COOKING TECHNIQUE
Collaborative learning, discussion, formative assessment, demonstration, and summative assessment

MAIN INGREDIENTS
☐ Computer access for each pair
☐ Google Form and corresponding spreadsheet
☐ Task cards (class set)
☐ Grading rubric

PREPARATION
Before the semester begins, create a Google Form and spreadsheet. Create two tabs in the Google spreadsheet (Formative, Summative). Test out the form, spreadsheet, and task cards with your instruction librarians. Print out a class set of task cards for each library classroom. Create a rubric tying specific learning outcomes to questions on the Google Form for use at the end of the semester.

MAIN COOKING TECHNIQUE
1. Students work in pairs to complete one task (1, 2, or 3). Each pair chooses an appropriate library database, finds one "good" source, and answers the questions about their source using the Google Form.
2. Display all responses on the spreadsheet. Ask students to report back to the class what they found, where they looked, and whether they had any problems finding it.
3. Based on formative assessment, the librarian can demonstrate the discovery tool, a database, library catalog, or reference database, as needed.
4. There are two tabs at the bottom of the Google spreadsheet: 1 (Formative Assessment) and 2 (Do Not Delete! Summative Assessment). After each class, copy from 1 to 2. Delete responses from 1.
5. At the end of the semester, select a random sample of responses from the Summative Assessment spreadsheet and grade them using the rubric.
6. Based on findings from using the rubric, make adjustments to the activity as necessary to address areas of confusion.

ALLERGY WARNINGS
- Encourage students to use their own topics, but provide sample topics for classes that visit the library early in the semester.
- Double-check your "Share" settings in the top right corner of the Google spreadsheet to make sure that all your librarians will be able to edit the spreadsheet.

- We embed our Google Forms into the course LibGuide and teach several classes at the same time. If you have multiple instruction classrooms, create one Google Form per classroom. Just make sure that the students use the correct form!

CHEF'S NOTE

Give students a broad type of information they need to find (i.e. background, scholarly analysis, etc.) instead of telling them which database to use. Don't spoon-feed them! It's okay if they stumble or fail. This activity always generates a good discussion of research strategies and it allows students to learn from each other. For longer classes, have students complete more than one task card. This is a very flexible instruction/assessment activity that can be adjusted to subject-specific classes. We revise the rubric annually and norm it during the summer.

ADDITIONAL RESOURCES

Using formative and summative assessments: http://bit.ly/tastetest2.

Setting the Table:
Using Ethnographic Methods to Understand First-Year Students
Ilka Datig, Nazareth College, Lorette Wilmot Library, Head of Instruction & Outreach, idatig5@naz.edu

NUTRITION INFORMATION
Ethnographic methods are useful for getting information about the worldview and mental models of the subject population. The goal of "Setting the Table" is to assess how first-year students view libraries, and what their previous experiences with libraries have been like.

The project involves a survey, administered to students before they arrive on campus, and interviews with first-year students within the first month of the academic year. This information can be used in first-year programming and instruction in a number of ways.

COOKING TIME
Ongoing

DIETARY GUIDELINES
Ethnography is becoming an increasingly popular method in library research and can be used to analyze and assess many different aspects of library services and design. This recipe is an example of using ethnographic methods to explore students' mental models of libraries.

MAIN COOKING TECHNIQUE
- Survey. Since the survey is likely to be very short and simple, this can be a basic Google Forms document. More advanced survey software, such as Qualtrics, could also be used.
- Interviews. If the librarian wants to be able to transcribe and thoroughly analyze the interviews, it is advisable to use an audio recorder.

MAIN INGREDIENTS
- ☐ Survey software (optional)
- ☐ Audio recording device
- ☐ Qualitative data analysis software (optional): If the librarian wants to perform deep analysis of the survey and interview responses, qualitative data analysis software, such as Atlas.ti or Nvivo, can be extremely useful.

PREPARATION
First, the librarian needs to design the survey and interview questions. Please see Figure 1 for possible ideas. The survey should be

---

FIGURE 1. SAMPLE QUESTIONS

Survey Questions:
1. Please describe your high school library.
2. What, in your opinion, are libraries for?

Interview Questions:
3. What was the library like in your previous school?
4. How did you use that library?
5. What other libraries do you have experience with?
6. What do you think libraries are for?
7. What do you think librarians do?
8. What expectations did you have for the [college/university name] library?
9. How do you plan to use the [college/university name] library, if at all?
10. Think back to your favorite library. How did it make you feel to walk into that library?
11. How do you feel when you walk in a library? Do you feel like you have to change your behaviors in any way?
12. If you're trying to study, what do you want the environment to be like?
13. How would you describe your ideal library?

---

short and simple, and the interview questions should be open-ended with room for reflection. Next, the librarian needs to work with the appropriate office on campus (perhaps Student Affairs or Admissions) to distribute the survey to first-year students during the summer before they arrive to begin classes.

The email should include a one- to two-sentence description and a link to the electronic survey. Students should be advised that the survey is short, sweet, and entirely optional. Librarians should be prepared to review survey responses and begin analyzing themes before classes begin.

MAIN COOKING METHOD

1. Implement the survey. Before a new academic year begins, ideally in June or July, the survey is sent out to incoming first-year students.
2. Review the results. The librarian can then spend time in August reviewing the results and beginning to form an understanding of how these students are planning on using the library. Some questions to keep in mind during this period: What themes are emerging from the data? Are students reporting bad experiences with libraries? Have some never used a library at all? Do they think of libraries places to study and learn, or just storage areas for books?
3. Conduct interviews. During the first month of classes, ideally in the second or third week, the librarian will need

to put out a call for interview subjects. It may be helpful to offer some sort of incentive for the participants' time. If the librarian is working alone, talking to 5–10 students is probably sufficient. If there are more potential interviewers, then that number can be increased. The interviews are an opportunity to expand on the knowledge gained from the survey. Librarians should dig deep into personal experiences and try to gain a rich picture of how the new students think about libraries.

4. Review the data. As soon as possible, the librarian should review all the data and see what themes and ideas emerge.
5. Adapt freshmen orientation and first-year instruction plans. When analyzing the data and making plans, here are some questions to keep in mind:
   a. Does the library need to emphasize the role of librarians beyond that of "book-shelvers"?
   b. Does it make sense to talk about the differences among high school, public, and academic libraries?
   c. Are there activities that can broaden the students' views of what libraries are for?
   d. Has the library gained any good ideas that might be used to improve the library space, services, or outreach plans?
6. Share results. The librarian should make sure to share the information gleaned

from this project with the rest of their colleagues. As students will be different every year, this project can be repeated yearly, every other year, or however else the librarian sees fit.

ALLERGY WARNINGS

- It can be difficult to find participants for interviews; the librarian may want to consider offering an incentive.

CHEF'S NOTE

- This project has been used with first-year international students and can be adapted for either (or both) groups, along with transfer students.
- This project is conducted over the summer and fall in order to get insight from first-year students before they are too heavily influenced by their new college/university library.
- This project can be supplemented in a number of ways: informal or formal observation of students' study habits (in the library and elsewhere on campus), photo diaries, and mental mapping. Please see Foster & Gibbons for more ideas. All of these methods can enrich the librarian's understanding of the first-year student library experience.
- Librarians who wish to publish or present on their findings should also work with their local Institutional Review Board while developing their survey and interview protocols.

ADDITIONAL RESOURCES

- Datig, Ilka. "What is a library?: International college students' perceptions of libraries." *The Journal of Academic Librarianship* 40.3 (2014): 350–356.
- Foster, Nancy Fried, and Susan L. Gibbons. *Studying Students: The Undergraduate Research Project at the University of Rochester.* Chicago, IL: ACRL, 2007.

Season to Taste:
Using Citation Analysis and Focus Groups to Assess First-Year Student Research Papers

Ilka Datig, Nazareth College, Lorette Wilmot Library, Head of Instruction & Outreach, idatig5@naz.edu

NUTRITION INFORMATION

Citation analysis is a well-established method in library research, and can be a very useful tool for assessing student work. When combined with qualitative methods, such as focus groups, it can help provide a rich picture of students' information literacy skills.

The goal of "Season to Taste" is to assess how first-year students find, evaluate, and use different types of information sources. This is achieved by systematically reviewing the sources that students use in their papers, in addition to talking to them about their process. This information can be used to develop and improve library instruction programs and outreach.

COOKING TIME

Ongoing

DIETARY GUIDELINES

This recipe is useful for assessing students' information literacy skills. It combines authentic assessment (review of actual research artifacts) with qualitative data. As such, it is an example of the usefulness of mixed methods for assessing student work and research behaviors. For best results, it should be integrated with other methods within a larger instructional assessment program.

MAIN COOKING TECHNIQUE

- Citation analysis. Citation analysis involves documenting and classifying each citation in a references list or bibliography according to pre-set criteria. The first order of business for this project is determining what student work should be analyzed. It would make sense to partner with a faculty member (or members) to identify opportunities for looking at first-year student research artifacts (such as original research papers or annotated bibliographies). The class does not necessarily have to have completed in a library instruction session; the data will be valuable to the library in any case. Most librarians embarking on citation analysis projects use either Microsoft Excel or Access to track the data.
- Focus groups. These should be scheduled as closely as possible to the students' due dates for their assignments. This will help to ensure that everything is still fresh in their minds. Focus groups allow students to hear each other's opinions and experiences; if confidentiality is important, interviews would also be a possibility. The sessions should be audio recorded, unless the librarian is confident in their ability to take very detailed notes.

MAIN INGREDIENTS

- ☐ Microsoft Excel or Access
- ☐ Audio recording device

PREPARATION

Before beginning the project, the librarian(s) involved need to consider what they want to measure and assess. There are a large number of variables that can be measured with citation analysis, including type of source, age, library availability, and subject area. The librarians will also need to decide if they are only reviewing the student bibliographies, or if they want to review how sources are cited in the body of the papers.

Although the latter method is more time-intensive, it provides great insight into how the sources from the bibliography are actually being used. The next item is preparing a list of questions for the focus groups. These questions should be open-ended and encourage reflection upon the research process. Please see Figure 1 for some possible ideas, which can be adapted to a variety of different situations.

FIGURE 1. FOCUS GROUP QUESTIONS

1. How did you find sources for your assignment?

2. Did you use any library resources, such as the catalog or databases? Can you explain that in detail?

3. How did you make the decision to include and exclude sources?

4. How important was reliability or trustworthiness to you?

5. How did you go about deciding if something was reliable?

6. What were some of the difficult parts of the process of finding sources?

7. Do you think you used any skills that you developed in a library instruction session?

MAIN COOKING METHOD

1. Identify an appropriate first-year course assignment to analyze, and collaborate with faculty to gain access.

2. Prepare focus group protocols and determine metrics for citation analysis.

3. Schedule the focus groups. Most research papers are due at the end of a semester, so it would make sense to schedule the focus groups during the finals period. Although students may be very busy at this time of year, they may also appreciate an opportunity to reflect on the work that they have recently completed. Depending upon the size of the class, it might be necessary to hold more than one focus group session.

4. Begin citation analysis. Collect and analyze the student research papers using the chosen criteria.

5. Start to analyze the data, keeping these issues in mind:

- What types of sources are students using?

- How are they finding sources? Are students using library tools to find sources, or just the free web?

- Do they think about the format of their sources (i.e. books, journal articles, etc.) or is that irrelevant to them?

- What qualities do students look for in a source? Are they thinking about date of publication, peer review, or other factors?

- How can this information be used to improve library instruction and outreach?

6. Share the results. The librarian should make sure to share the information gleaned from this project with the faculty partner, as well as the rest of their colleagues. This project can be applied iteratively, either with the same class or with another first-year course.

ALLERGY WARNINGS

It can be difficult to get students to participate in focus groups; librarians should consider offering incentives and make sure that the times are convenient to students.

CHEF'S NOTE

- This project is flexible and can be adapted for use with any student group.

- Librarians interested in measuring the effect of library instruction on first-year students can consider using a control group.

- There is a large amount of library literature on applying citation analysis to the assessment of library instruction. Please see the Additional Resources section for more ideas.

- Librarians who wish to publish or present on their findings should also work with their local Institutional Review Board while developing their protocols.

ADDITIONAL RESOURCES

- Clark, Sarah, and Susan Chinburg. 2010. "Research Performance in Undergraduates Receiving Face to Face Versus Online Library Instruction: A Citation Analysis." *Journal of Library Administration* 50 (5–6): 530–542.

- Cooke, Rachel, and Danielle Rosenthal. 2011. "Students Use More Books After Library Instruction: An Analysis of Undergraduate Paper Citations." *College & Research Libraries* 72 (4): 332–343.

- Hoffmann, Kristin and Lise Doucette. 2012. "A Review of Citation Analysis Methodologies for Collection Management." *College & Research Libraries* 73 (4): 321–335.

The Ingredients for Assessing a Personal Librarian Program for First-Year Students

Eric Resnis, Organizational Effectiveness Specialist, Miami University, eric.resnis@miamioh.edu; Jennifer Natale, Assistant Professor and Liaison Librarian, Appalachian State University, natalejj@appstate.edu

NUTRITION INFORMATION

The idea of a Personal Librarian has gained considerable traction, with a notable amount of colleges and universities using Personal Librarians to increase and/or supplement outreach efforts to first-year students. Personal Librarianship aims to foster relationships beyond the point-of-need with a focus on sustained communication between the librarian and students.

As the landscape shifts toward the demonstration of value and impact, assessment of a Personal Librarian program seeks to answer several important questions: How do we determine if this program is a valuable use of resources? How do we know if this program is impactful to students? This recipe will help you to assess your program with data you already collect to determine if your efforts are making a difference.

COOKING TIME

Assessment of a Personal Librarian program should be completed on an ongoing basis, with analysis and reporting occurring at the end of an academic year. This allows enough time to plan and implement change in the following years of the program. Continually collecting data allows you to eventually look at the impact of the program on students over multiple years.

DIETARY GUIDELINES

Oftentimes, assessment of outreach programs is primarily based on attendance or student perceptions of the program. That information can be helpful, but the questions that can be answered from that data are limited. This recipe describes a data collection procedure that helps determine if a key outcome of a Personal Librarian program is being met: increased library engagement. The outcome is common to many outreach programs, and a similar procedure could be used for assessing those programs as well.

MAIN COOKING TECHNIQUE

This assessment plan is primarily based on user engagement and utilizes data sources that already exist. For each data source (or main ingredient), one usage/checkout is defined as one engagement. Engagement numbers are collected for the academic year. The data is then analyzed to answer the following questions:
- Are students with a Personal Librarian engaging with the library?
- Is the library engagement of Personal Librarian students significantly different from those who do not have a Personal Librarian?
- Do Personal Librarian students show engagement in a particular area?
- Is there a clear relationship between email engagement and library usage?

MAIN INGREDIENTS

The data sources utilized for assessment may include the following:
- ☐ Number of checkouts of library materials
- ☐ Number of study room reservations
- ☐ Number of student reading room entrances
- ☐ Number of computer logins
- ☐ Number of student consultations recorded by Personal Librarians
- ☐ Number of library workshops attended
- ☐ Other data you have that indicates use of library space and services where the student name is collected. Anonymous data will not work for this assessment technique.

Note that for the above methods, collection will depend highly on the systems that your library has in place. Check carefully to see what your data collection systems are capable of providing to you, and if you need to implement new systems before this procedure can begin.

For this assessment process to work smoothly, it is also suggested that you contact students using email marketing software. The software tracks whether students are opening your email, how many times they open it (if students revisit the email later in the semester), and if students are clicking any links to information you provide in the email. Depending on the number of students you are engaging, many options are available, including fee-based options (Constant Contact), free options with upgrades (MailChimp, Benchmark), and entirely free options (Boomerang).

PREPARATION

Identify your list of students who have a Personal Librarian and a control group of students who do not. Generate a list of the main ingredients that you want to collect. Create a method for collecting data where one doesn't already exist—for example, collecting the names of students who attend workshops or the number of interactions with a Personal Librarian. Determine what program, such as Excel, you will use to collect the data for later analysis.

MAIN COOKING METHOD

1. Determine what data sources you will be utilizing. Ensure that you are able to collect the type of data that you need from the source. Don't make assumptions about the data that is available or how it is presented.
2. Make a plan for collection of the data. Some items might be collected monthly, while others yearly. We suggest that you do not wait until the end of the academic year to collect the data.
3. Create a secure location to house the data. Share with collaborators, if you have them.
4. Determine your sample of students to assess. Depending on the number of students in a Personal Librarian program, assessment of the entire group or a random sample may occur (at least 20 percent suggested). A random sample can be generated in Excel using the "RANDBETWEEN" function. For comparison purposes, we suggest also having a sample of similar students who do not have a Personal Librarian.
5. During the academic year, do periodic check-ins to ensure that your sources are collecting data correctly.
6. At the end of the academic year, compile and analyze your data. Use a spreadsheet that contains the students being assessed in rows, and data from your sources in the columns.
7. Look at the data to make comparisons between students who have a Personal Librarian and those who do not. Areas that may be examined (but not limited to) include:
   - Total number of engagements during the academic year
   - Average number of engagements during the academic year
   - Engagement compared to email open rates (if you use email marketing software)
   - In-person engagement versus online engagement
8. Discuss the findings with your group of Personal Librarians and the library staff as a whole. Use the discussion and data to create an action plan for improvement of the program during the next academic year.

ALLERGY WARNINGS

- Please note that this assessment method does require student tracking, and you may need approval from your Institutional Review Board to complete the project.
- To protect the privacy of your students, only capture usage, such as checkouts or computer logins, and not the nature of the usage (specific items checked out or software used).
- Note that, depending on your data collection system, you may need to collect data individually for each student. When compiling your data, pulling together disparate data sets may also take considerable time and effort. Plan ahead and think about this when forming the project.

CHEF'S NOTE

Be inquisitive! Is there a question you have that your data might answer? A high-level view of engagement with the library is important to assess, but you may also want to look at your data to determine if there is a difference on a specific variable between students with a Personal Librarian and those without. For example, if you promoted workshops specifically to Personal Librarian students, were they more likely to attend? Once you have concluded the assessment, share the results with others in your library to discuss and consider changes for future iterations.

First-Year Student Ceviche:
Turning Raw Ingredients into a Spicy Dish

Corrine Syster, Harrisburg Area Community College, Reference and Instruction Librarian, ccsyster@hacc.edu; Allyson Valentine, Reference and Instruction Librarian, Harrisburg Area Community College, afvalent@hacc.edu

NUTRITION INFORMATION

A library exploration assignment is included with the First-Year Experience (FYE) course and is intended to get new students familiar with the layout, materials (both physical and online), and people within the space. Based on feedback from faculty, the assignment moved from a scavenger hunt to an open-ended question format that asked students to reflect upon their experience in the library and using its website.

The exploration activity focuses on how the students might use the library in their future courses and asks students to evaluate and identify resources that would be most important to their success. After collecting the completed assignments, librarians can categorize the students' open-ended qualitative responses into analyzable quantitative information, making it easier to share the results.

COOKING TIME

15–30 minutes for activity (depending on size of library); additional time for cooking the assignment and serving results

DIETARY GUIDELINES

As a community college, the students in our sample come from a wide variety of back-grounds, including non-traditional and international students. We tried to keep that in mind as we created our questions, since some of our students have limited experience with libraries. We chose to encourage students to focus on reflection and personal interpretations rather than the "correct" answer.

This allows students to generate meaningful connections to the library as opposed to simply transferring trivial information to a sheet of paper. It is especially important to encourage first-year students to think about how the library contributes to their success in college. This assignment could easily be adapted to be meaningful for online-only students by focusing on the library's online presence.

ACRL FRAMEWORKS ADDRESSED

- Research as Inquiry
- Searching as Strategic Exploration

MAIN COOKING TECHNIQUE

Independent exploration of library space and resources

MAIN INGREDIENTS

- ☐ Library exploration assignments
- ☐ Spreadsheet software
- ☐ Word processing software

PREPARATION

- ☐ Create a library assignment with open-ended questions that allow students to make their own judgments about the library. Examples:
  - » Explore the library and find something that you are less familiar with or something that confuses you (examples: equipment and a sign, a space). Describe it to the best of your abilities, and try to explain how you think someone might use it.
  - » Locate a place where a library staff member is available for help. Spend a few minutes observing (from a polite distance!) their interactions with other students. What are they helping the students do? If after a few minutes there are no students being helped, you may ask one of the library employees how they help people. Write a few sentences about what kind of help is offered at the library.
  - » Spend a few minutes exploring the library space. Feel free to peek in rooms, look at the shelves, and observe what kind of places there might be for students to work in or what kind of things a student could

147

use. Write about two things you think would be useful to you as a college student.

» Think about what you learned about the college library today. What was different or surprising about this library compared to libraries you have used in the past?

» Write about one thing you learned today that you think will help you be a successful student. Be sure to write what it is and how it will help you.

☐ Determine your distribution and collection methods for the completed assignments.

☐ Optional: Connect with faculty in the program for feedback on questions.

COOKING METHOD

1. Either as part of an instruction session or prior to class, have students explore the library and complete the assignment.

2. Collect the completed assignments (or have copies made, if instructors are using them for a course grade) and give each assignment an identification number.

3. Read through the assignments and identify common or main themes for each question based on the questions in the Preparation section above. Several students mention help with printing, computers, photocopying, which are different from a group that mentions finding a book, helping with citations, or finding an article.

4. Create a "code" (a phrase similar to a subject heading) for the answers that correspond with the themes you have identified—e.g., "IT help" as a code for all the answers that describe help with printing, software, photocopiers, wireless, etc.

5. To enter data into a spreadsheet, there are two options:

» Open up your spreadsheet and create column labels for the identification number and each question and/or identified code. If there are multiple codes assigned to question 1, you might have a column labeled "1. IT Help" and "1. Reference." Then enter the information for each assignment into the rows. As long as you know what these labels refer to, the naming convention is up to you.

» Recommended: Create a Google Form to reflect the kind of information you want to gather and then submit one form for each assignment. You will want to ensure that the Google Form is set to create a Google Sheet to capture the responses. (It will be a file labeled with the title of your form followed by "(Responses)".)

6. Once the data is entered, you can insert a "Pivot Table," which will summarize your responses automatically. This feature is available in all spreadsheet software, but can be found in various locations. You will get a blank table and

a place to specify which row, column, and values you are interested in analyzing.

» The pivot table will give you numbers, but feel free to add some spice by inserting a chart based on that data.

ALLERGY WARNINGS

• Processed in a facility that uses math. May contain percentages and calculations. Several printed and online resources are available to describe coding, pivot tables, and basic data analysis and visualization in further detail.

• Remember to taste along the way and ask others for input. Some questions may seem very straightforward, yet are worded in a way that give unexpected results or vary too much to be meaningful.

CHEF'S NOTE

The benefit of this assignment and assessment is that it helps both the library and the student reflect on the library's resources before entering the classroom/library session. We encourage instructors to give this assignment to students early in the semester so students can identify and become comfortable with library support and resources early in their first semester. The collection and analysis of this information can be used to provide the library with important feedback about student use of resources and space as well as their comfort level.

After analyzing and organizing the results of the exploration assignment, we shared them at library department meetings and discussed the challenges and perceptions of students coming into our library. We used that discussion to brainstorm ways we could better serve our students, and to highlight and describe our collections. Each campus evaluated their signage, collections, resources, and spaces, based on student feedback on what confused them or what they were less familiar with. Some changes included one campus purchasing display supplies to highlight subjects with the call number areas. One campus is eliminating their reference collection and reorganizing their library space. Several campuses changed signage around the library. For example, we discovered that a sign we used to label a computer as having a specific program was misleading for anyone who did not know what that program was. We've since relocated the computer and reworded the sign to make it more straightforward.

The data gathered on what students identified as changes that would be most helpful to them is being used to highlight resources in other classes, in faculty orientations, in advertising and promotional materials, as well as campus tours, etc. Though we had already begun a redesign of the library website, the results of the question where we asked students to choose links on our website to explore, gave us feedback about where on the page students were most likely to click on links and what informa-

tion they were most interested in. We then highlighted resources in our newly designed website that we felt were most important to students. We also shared the results of our assessment in a foundational studies discipline meeting with the instructors who teach our FYE courses. We felt that this helped them understand students' challenges, concerns, and experiences, and allows us to better brainstorm and collaborate together for student success. We then took recommendations from foundational studies discipline to make improvements and changes to assignment back to the library dept.

Surprises: Students can't write a response that answers multiple questions; quiet study space is very important to them; and many students have had very different experiences with libraries in their past.

Takeaways: We found that our students were consistently surprised and pleased that there were people who were friendly, willing, and available to help them. All of this can help us better prepare a student-centered instruction session, think about how we organize our physical and online spaces, and help us provide the services that best suit our students. Though our students were overwhelmingly able to identify us as helpful and as a place to get resources, many pointed out that our libraries are very different than the ones they have used in the past. This gave us good insight on some of the challenges our students face and their

lack of familiarity with library resources or research. A sizable percentage of students identified the library as a place to study and use computers. The space is really important to the demographic we work with, since so many are non-traditional and we're a commuting college.

Personal experience with assessment: While we wanted our assignment to be reflective, our first go at creating open-ended questions made it very difficult to assess. We realized that in the written reflection portion of the assignment, we were really asking students to answer four questions instead of one, and some of those questions were redundant. This led to several students only responding to parts of the prompt. No single student addressed all four parts of the question. We had to change the question language and break apart the questions into separate questions.

ADDITIONAL RESOURCES:
- The first version of our assignment: http://tinyurl.com/originalassignment.
- Our assessment report: http://tinyurl.com/FS100report.
- Revised version of our assignment after assessment: http://tinyurl.com/assignmentrevised.